THE VIDEO CONNECTION

Integrating Video into Language Teaching

Rick Altman
The University of Iowa

HOUGHTON MIFFLIN COMPANY   BOSTON

Dallas / Geneva, Illinois / Palo Alto / Princeton, New Jersey

Video stills are reproduced with the permission of:
Radio Televisión Española, *Ni en vivo ni en directo,* pages 71, 82. The
Project for International Communication Studies, *La Porcelaine à Limoges*
(Centre National de Documentation Pédagogique), page 13; *Un Village
se met à table* (Centre National de Documentation Pédagogique), pages
16, 17; *Little Red Riding Hood* [Perrault and Grimm versions] (The Project
for International Communication Studies), pages 34, 158; *Télé-douzaine*
(Antenne 2 – The Project for International Communication Studies),
pages 39, 102; *Télématin* (Antenne 2 – The Project for International
Communication Studies), pages 49, 50, 52, 69, 97, 111 right; *Nachrichten
I* (British Broadcasting Corporation – The Project for International Communication Studies), page 61; *Fleuve Sénégal* (Institut pour la Coopération
Audiovisuelle Francophone), page 81; *La Main dans le sac* (Centre National
de Documentation Pédagogique), page 94; *Telejournal* (British Broadcasting
Corporation – The Project for International Communication Studies),
page 111, left; *Sécurité Routière* (Centre National de Documentation Pédagogique), page 156; *ABC der Wirtschaft* (Eurotel – The Project for
International Communication Studies), page 166.

Drawings: Anco/Boston Inc.

Printed in the U.S.A.

ISBN: 0-395-48143-0

Library of Congress Catalog Card Number: 88-81317
  BCDEFGHIJ-DH-9543210-89

CONTENTS

PREFACE

For decades, educators proclaimed television to be a promising teaching device. From the fifties to the early seventies, book after book assured us that the era of remote classrooms, telecourses, and videocassette recorders was just around the corner. To the surprise of many, and the delight of more than a few doubters, that corner was never fully turned. Although "Sesame Street" and a few other educational programs may have had a significant impact on elementary education, the video medium, until recently, has had less influence on higher education.

Foreign language teachers, in particular, were skeptical about the educational prospects of the small screen. During the seventies and early eighties, this attitude was understandable, given the inauthentic nature of most available foreign-language television programs in this country. The technological incompatibility of U.S. and European television systems also presented a nearly insurmountable barrier. Neither the possibility of using American-made video materials that lacked authenticity nor the option of falling back on the use of foreign films, which were characteristically lengthy, linguistically difficult, and awkward to manipulate, seemed to be viable solutions.

The growth of the videocassette recorder market has rapidly changed many instructors' attitude toward video. Where once the only option was the lockstep approach of the telecourse, now teachers can choose their own materials, tailoring specific programs to their individual needs. The video revolution has been extraordinarily slow, however, in reaching foreign language education. Authentic foreign language video materials have only recently become available to the U.S. market in significant number.

In response, language teachers are now hurrying to equip their language laboratories and classrooms with video equipment and to experiment with the best methods for incorporating foreign video materials into their teaching.

As codirector of the Project for International Communication Studies (PICS), a nonprofit distributor of international video materials located at the University of Iowa, I have had the opportunity to view firsthand the growing interest in foreign language video pedagogy. Typically, instructors come to PICS with two questions. After inquiring "What materials do you have?", they invariably ask "How do you use them?" Since video pedagogy is a new field, instructors understandably feel the need for some guidance.

The foreign language profession needs a short, *practical* book on the use of video materials for the teaching of language and culture. Besides laying an appropriate theoretical foundation for a new video pedagogy, this book should provide practical suggestions for the use of video at all levels. It cannot avoid technological and legal topics, but it must somehow treat them in readable, accessible English. At the same time, such a book should provide well-founded, practical recommendations for establishing video facilities, as well as current information on available video programs. This is the book I have proposed to write.

The Video Connection is intended for foreign language instructors at all levels who are using video equipment and materials for the first time, students in methodology courses, and more advanced video users searching for new ways in which to use video. My own fondest hope is that this book will contribute in a significant way to the widespread acceptance of the increasingly sophisticated video pedagogy that is currently being created around the country.

I would like to thank the following reviewers for their useful comments and suggestions during the development of this book: Rita Goldberg, St. Lawrence University; Randall L. Jones, Brigham Young University; Edward C. Knox, Middlebury College; Katherine D. Lawrence, The University of Maryland, College Park; Charles P. Richardson, Ohio University, Athens; Sharon Guinn Scinicariello, Case Western Reserve University; David F. Stout, Austin College.

Without the support of my colleagues at PICS, this book could not have been written. My thanks thus go to Jackie Ferdig and Susan Redfern, to Deb Bjornstad and Susan Skoglund, to Sue Otto, Janet Altman, and Jim Pusack. I also wish to thank an enlightened individual, a man who from the start understood the potential importance of international video, and whose support made PICS possible: University of Iowa Vice President for Research and Development, Duane C. Spriestersbach.

R.A.

PART I

General Principles

CHAPTER 1
Video and Language Acquisition Theory

What does video have to offer to language education? Can video contribute equally to divergent methods? How do currently influential theories look from the point of view of video? Does video have any contribution of its own to make to current theoretical debates? Even in a practical book, it is appropriate to begin with broad questions such as these.

The goals and techniques of language teaching depend heavily on our definition of language. How does language work? What are the relative roles played by the oral and written versions of language? To what extent and in what way are language and culture interrelated? Before any of these questions can be answered, a still more important question must be confronted. How do we understand language at all? What are the processes that lead to understanding? What role might video play in facilitating comprehension?

The Process of Comprehension

In recent years, increasing attention has been paid to the process of comprehension and its importance in language acquisition. In particular, the influential theories of Stephen D. Krashen and their practical application in Tracy D. Terrell's Natural Approach have popularized the notion, previously advanced by the Direct Method and other related approaches, that language acquisition depends primarily on consumption of massive doses of "comprehensible input." By comprehensible input, Krashen and Terrell mean target language speech or texts that include challenging yet comprehensible portions.[1] Simply by reading and listening to appropriately chosen samples of the target language, the theory claims, even beginners can make rapid progress in their ability to understand and eventually produce the language. How this process takes place is less clear. Why does comprehensible input make such an important contribution? What mechanisms lead from input to comprehension? And just what constitutes comprehension?

In spite of increased attention to the oral language over the last decade, most current approaches to teaching continue to work with a fundamentally fixed, printed model of language. This model is built on the belief that there is a single sanctioned version of the language; it emphasizes attentiveness to grammatical accuracy, consistent presentation of words according to printed standards (that is, separated by spaces), and an approach to vocabulary building that depends heavily on English equivalents. We might usefully diagram this familiar model in the following way:

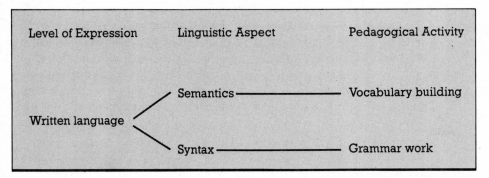

Level of Expression	Linguistic Aspect	Pedagogical Activity
Written language	Semantics	Vocabulary building
	Syntax	Grammar work

Two main assumptions characterize this traditional model. First, it is assumed that the target language is made up of discrete words constituting individual units of meaning that can be conveniently defined by familiar equivalents in the form of either line drawings or English words. Second, the organization of separate words into full sentences is assumed to depend on the principles of prescriptive grammar.

At first blush, it might seem that the familiar but outmoded grammar-translation method is being described here. Far from it. Even the most advanced of the recent Natural Approach textbooks, *Dos Mundos,* by Terrell *et al.,* is replete with translated single-word vocabulary lists and makes little effort to recognize the special conventions of oral language. Often called "mistakes" when they appear in the written context, the varied expressions and constructions of the oral language nevertheless remain central to a language.

Video challenges us to base our linguistic model on oral language and the target culture as well as on written language. Video reminds us that language is first constituted by *sounds* and only then represented by letters. Before becoming separate and discrete, words are experienced as part of a sound continuum that can be understood only after the process of *segmentation* is complete. Video's unique audiovisual combination reminds us that *semantics* is not limited to translation; true understanding of individual words depends not on the establishment of English equivalents but on the understanding of a word's range of uses within the target language. At the same time, the variety of language registers present in authentic foreign video materials demonstrates that comprehension depends less on knowledge of a single, narrow, prescriptive grammar than on understanding of a broad, descriptive grammar corresponding to the varied *syntax* characteristic of actual usage. By displaying language in context, video also shows that the meaning of specific words or utterances varies according to the speaker's identity and situation, hence the importance of recognizing the *systems of discourse* employed by a particular language. Video never allows us to forget that full understanding depends on our ability to perceive the reciprocal relationship between the language and the *systems of culture* that it defines and by which it is simultaneously defined.

Examining language through the culturally specific audiovisual medium of foreign video radically changes our model of language. In a new, video-influenced model, the traditional model's single level of expression grows to three different levels, each giving rise to separate linguistic aspects. Each aspect in turn presents a potential impediment to comprehension and thus calls for a discrete pedagogical activity. A diagram of the new model looks like the following:

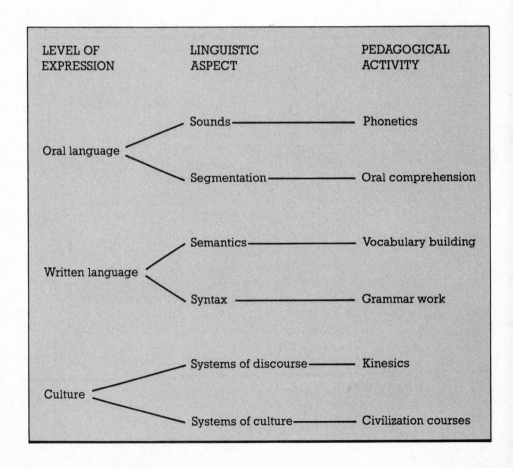

LEVEL OF EXPRESSION	LINGUISTIC ASPECT	PEDAGOGICAL ACTIVITY
Oral language	Sounds	Phonetics
	Segmentation	Oral comprehension
Written language	Semantics	Vocabulary building
	Syntax	Grammar work
Culture	Systems of discourse	Kinesics
	Systems of culture	Civilization courses

According to this new model, the three levels of linguistic expression are fundamentally and inalterably interdependent. In order to understand individual words, the model suggests, we must be able to recognize specific sounds and to properly segment the continuous flow of sound; yet we cannot divide the sounds into words unless we can recognize and make sense of individual words. Similarly, we are unable to understand even single words unless we know how they are used by the target culture, and yet we understand that culture largely by apprehending the way in which it molds and deploys language.

Comparing simple outlines of the traditional model and the new video-inspired model fails to demonstrate the extraordinary differences between them. The differences can best be illustrated by a graphic display of the ways in which each system operates.

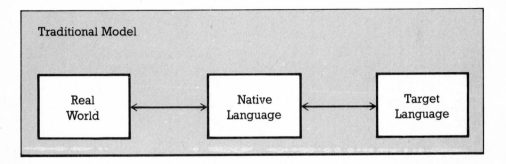

Traditional Model

Real World ⟷ Native Language ⟷ Target Language

With the traditional model, comprehension of the target language is filtered through the student's native language and that culture's characteristic apprehension of the real world. This familiar method thus fails to grasp the target culture's particular understanding of the real world. A video-inspired model places far greater importance on both the oral target language and the target culture's unique apprehension of the real world. According to the video-inspired model, students of a language gain comprehension not through the filter of their native language and culture but through repeated recognition of the relationship between the oral and written versions of the target language and the target culture's apprehension of the real world.

The process of comprehension can involve each of the six linguistic aspects (the six "S's") diagrammed on page 4: sounds, segmentation, semantics, syntax, systems of discourse, and systems of culture. Each of these concerns must also be addressed in our teaching and our teaching materials. What combination of materials might best be able to serve this broader pedagogy? Clearly, the most appropriate materials must provide access not only to the written language but also to the spoken language and to the culture at large. Even more important, the materials

Video-inspired Model

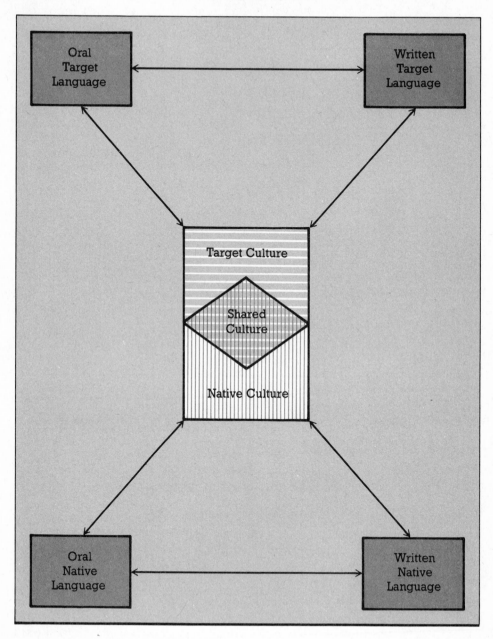

must reveal the *relationship* among these three areas, for it is through recognition of that relationship that the student reaches understanding.

Where might we look for sources of comprehensible input that maximize the relationship between language and the real world? In the past a great deal of weight has been placed on classroom discussion. On the best days, classroom discussion and teacher talk provide acceptable, comprehensible input. More often, however, student speech involves idiosyncracies and errors different from those typically encountered in the target culture. Furthermore, even the teacher may have a hard time connecting the target language to the real world as experienced by native speakers of the target language. Students hear **finestra, ventana,** or **fenêtre** and imagine something with a screen and a shade that goes up and down, or maybe even a car window, whereas in Italy, Spain, and France these words invoke a totally different mental picture.

One important advance in creating materials appropriate to a new pedagogy sensitive to culture and oral language was provided by James J. Asher's Total Physical Response (TPR) method. Recognizing that the human body offers an important connection between cultures, Asher uses oral, body-related imperatives to initiate students into language comprehension and production. Students' attention is thus easily concentrated on the relationship between the spoken language and the real world, without any intervention of their native language. By emphasizing the body and other familiar objects and actions, TPR gives students a steady source of connections between the target language and the corresponding objects and activities.

If TPR works, it is clearly because it insists on using language in context, always providing not only the words but also the corresponding actions. Furthermore, as Krashen has pointed out, Asher's own research shows that students who only *observe* a TPR session perform as well as those who participate in the class.[2] This is an important point. Students are learning not primarily from engaging in a physical activity but from the process of identifying words with the corresponding physical objects or activities. Research on TPR, then, demonstrates that students of a foreign language need consistent observation of language/world connections more than they need direct experience of those connections. TPR is so successful at providing comprehensible input because it consistently furnishes both the language and the objects or actions to which the language refers. As with other audiovisual methods, TPR's visual activity anchors the oral word, and vice versa. TPR suffers, however, from the limitations that classroom teaching imposes: within the classroom it is difficult to broaden sufficiently the range of connections that students are called upon to make. With video, however, the classroom can easily be stretched to include an ever-expanding range of audiovisual relationships.

Context and Control

Video is extraordinarily well suited to display the connections between language and the real world upon which comprehension depends. Video's striking ability to make these connections stems from its unique combination of two nearly antithetical qualities: *maximum contextualization* and *maximum control*.

Theorists have long understood the importance of contextualization for the comprehension of written and oral language.[3] Numerous studies have shown that the process of comprehension includes an interaction between the text at hand and the subject's own prior organization of knowledge. Whether the texts are oral or written, whether they are composed in a first or a second language, individuals must form their expectations about future messages based on what they have understood so far. These expectations will in turn impinge on the individuals' understanding of the remainder of the message. Thus an ESL student reading a passage describing events that take place at high tea in an English country manor will rapidly form a pattern of expectation regarding messages still to come. These expectations will, of course, differ according to the subject's previous experience of high tea and English country manors.

Individuals who invoke the appropriate context of high tea are vastly aided in their understanding of the passage. Correctly anticipating the general characteristics of the parts of the text still to come (vocabulary, level of speech, social relationships, and the like), they are less likely to miss major aspects of the text than are, for example, listeners who expect the story to be about a six-year-old Californian's birthday party. The question is not *whether* people will posit some context but *which* context they will invoke. The better people are at recognizing the appropriate set of contexts and necessary revisions as they move through the text, the more likely they are to understand the text in question.

By and large, research devoted to the role of context in language learning has been based on the use of a single-medium text, usually either oral or written, more rarely image-based. Comprehension is seen to depend solely on the interaction of the text at hand and the subject's prior knowledge. Practical recommendations based on context-oriented research have tended to stress the importance of manipulating prior knowledge in order to ensure that subjects invoke an appropriate context. Of particular interest here are studies revealing the importance of visual materials for identifying appropriate contexts.[4] It has been repeatedly demonstrated that even a single line drawing that provides only a very general indication of the contents of a passage can have a marked effect on comprehension, if it is shown to subjects before they read or listen to the passage. Surprisingly, even pictures only vaguely related to a passage aid comprehension more than prior access to a list of the actual vocabulary words employed in the passage.[5]

Were these studies not so strongly tied to reading and the written language, their authors would no doubt have rapidly moved beyond a model assuming that subjects develop schemata for message processing solely on the basis of prior knowledge and the linguistic text. It seems obvious that any oral message will produce schemata dependent on the speaker's tone of voice, body language, and simultaneous activities. Thus, the familiar schema-theory model (prior knowledge and linguistic text) may be replaced with a three-part model (prior knowledge, linguistic text, and nonlinguistic signals). As any language learner knows, this added nonlinguistic channel is often paramount in the process of understanding. A difficult message can be made accessible with no more than a few hand signals that confirm or modify the contextualizing indicators provided by the text itself. The three-part model and the triangulation that it encourages are widely recognized by the general public as essential to the process of language learning. Books for children are always picture books; story time at the public library always combines acting with reading. Centuries of texts aimed at a semiliterate populace have combined visual and written texts. Monumental sculpture, block books, popular theater, illustrated novels, comics, cinema, and television all assure full comprehension through one medium's reinforcement of another.

Our objective here is not limited to maximizing comprehension, however. We must instead discover the methods and models that will most effectively maximize language acquisition in general. It seems quite clear that the multimedia-based text is destined to play an important part in this endeavor. By providing a culturally correct visual dictionary to support the verbal or written language, the multimedia-based text assures continued improvement of the subject's schema choice.

The various multimedia forms are not equally suitable to all language-learning tasks. For example, as children grow, the proportion of their books devoted to pictures diminishes, and adults are expected to be able to handle the written text alone, without visual support. So it is with second-language acquisition. Beginning students require a high level of redundancy between the language and its visual support (hand signals, blackboard drawings, textbook illustrations, and the like), whereas advanced students need redundancy only when they are moving into an unknown area. Multimedia texts appropriate to second-language teaching must also avoid visual oversimplification if they are to achieve the desired effect of familiarizing students with the real world associated with another language.

The contextualizing capacity of well-chosen video materials is striking.

Not only does the video medium provide an easily accessible combination of high-quality visual and aural material, but it has the capacity to provide—through visual and aural channels alike—extremely faithful renditions of the world associated with the target language. A high level of redundancy between linguistic message and visual material can thus be established through video materials when necessary with no consequent loss of authenticity. In contrast, illustrated books and theatrical presentations systematically reduce the real world to a point at which it is hardly recognizable, and most oral situations lose in authenticity of discursive situation what they gain in body language contextualization. By providing constant contextual updating, the video text not only maximizes comprehension of particular passages but also offers the potential to teach the linguistic and contextualizing skills needed for understanding all similar future passages in the target language, whether presented in video's multimedia format or not.

In addition to maximum contextualization, video provides maximum control over the linguistic content. The problem with most foreign-language situations that provide a reasonably high level of contextualization is that they are only minimally predictable. For example, authentic experiences in other countries provide a high level of contextualization. Asking for directions in a foreign country might elicit many responses: hand signals to indicate left and right, verbal indications matched by road signs and landmarks, or oral language doubled by body language. However, it is impossible to control the level of language input in authentic situations.

The instructor trying to provide students with authentic conversational input soon finds many pitfalls: new vocabulary, unattested grammatical forms, slang and regionalisms, acronyms and political or commercial jargon, local in-jokes and references to national history. Of course, students should be taught to handle most of these difficulties eventually, but the instructor must retain some degree of control over the rate of introduction of new challenges. The same problem constantly surfaces in the traditional classroom as well. The most interesting answers to the familiar question, "What did you do last night/weekend/summer/vacation?" are invariably those for which the class is least prepared.

Unlike authentic experiences in other countries, video materials strike a good balance between context and control. Unlike conversation, or even teacher talk or television, video is perfectly predictable if previewed. The instructor knows what is on the tape and can thus easily develop exercises that enhance comprehension or retention. There is no question which information is accompanied by full visual and oral redundancy and which may need special preparation in order to ensure comprehension. Instructors know which phrases are poorly enunciated and which are slang, dialect, or legalese. Passages that are clearly too difficult for the current level of class understanding can be removed or summarized. Instructors can thus predict where and why students will have trouble and plan accordingly. Krashen affirms that a steady dose of comprehensible input will lead to language acquisition. He recognizes, however, the difficulty of assuring comprehensibility. It is relatively easy to prepare written texts aimed for the right level, but oral material is harder to control. The predictability of video allows the instructor to prepare students in such a way that the video program will always be challenging and yet largely comprehensible.

Video Connections

The high level of control permitted by the video medium makes it possible to plan ahead in order to exploit fully any aspect of video. The breadth of contextualization available through video guarantees the instructor's ability to establish any of the connections necessary for comprehension. Much of this book is devoted to showing how these connections may be exploited through the use of video. Before practical considerations are offered, however, some preliminary remarks are needed on the types of connection that video is especially suited to make. This chapter has already distinguished six fundamental aspects of language that must be addressed in the language-teaching process. These six S's will serve as our guide to video connections (see page 4).

Sounds

Traditional language pedagogy based on a written model of language largely ignores the problem of sounds. To be sure, students are taught to make the sounds necessary for target-language production. However, since most target-language input takes place in the classroom, students tend to adopt the accents of those they hear most often: the teacher and fellow students, with perhaps a minor contribution from the voices on language-laboratory audiotapes. When these students arrive in a foreign country, such as Italy, they are immediately disconcerted by the range of accents encountered: not just Florentine and Neapolitan pronunciation, for example, but Venetian and Sicilian as well, not to mention the accents of North African and Yugoslavian immigrants, along with French and German tourists. By stressing production of so-called standard language sounds alone we do our students the disservice of denying them the ability to *recognize* supposedly nonstandard sounds. Worse, we often convince beginning students that their inability to produce particular sounds places them somehow beyond the limits of the target language's range of acceptability. Must pronunciation be Castilian? What about Argentinian and Cuban? Must it be peninsular Spanish? What about Peruvian, Mexican, and Chicano? But how can we possibly introduce our students to a broad range of *real* Spanish unless we can offer them both the sounds of the language and a sense of the visual context in which these sounds are used?

Differences in sounds are not just a question of regionalism. For example, individuals display different speech patterns at different stages of their lives. Not everyone can enunciate like a radio announcer, certainly not the timid twelve-year-old or the old person missing many teeth. Consider the impact of foreigners on High German. What does one do about the **Gastarbeiter** [foreign workers], the Luxemburgers, and the foreign EEC officials? It seems clear that our teaching must respect the variety of sounds through which German or any other language may be communicated.

Video makes the connections necessary for solving this problem. First, authentic international video programs can provide any desired diversity of sounds. Second, video programs reveal the range of sounds produced by individual speakers in differing situations. While not a high priority for introductory courses, this concern should be paramount at upper levels. Third, video matches sounds both to bodies and to contexts. Sounds come more easily to students who see sounds being produced by whole bodies. Fourth, video shows the sublingual sounds that never appear on the printed page but are perhaps a given language's single most unique attribute. Grunts, interjections, and seemingly nonsensical syllables carry an enormous amount of meaning in the oral world of most languages. Without them, students miss an important and engaging aspect of the target language.

Segmentation

To my mind, the process of segmentation constitutes the very heart of language comprehension. It is the learner's first problem, since no comprehension is possible without at least minimal segmentation. It also constitutes the learner's last problem, since segmentation of an unsegmented linguistic continuum can be completed only after phonetic, semantic, syntactic, discursive, and cultural analysis has taken place. For this reason, segmentation is certainly the most difficult task that a student must face, and the one task that textbooks and instructors almost never consider directly. The difficulty of segmenting the oral language is compounded by the traditional tendency to teach the written language first and only then to encourage students to recognize and produce oral sounds. By the time most students receive any significant amount of authentic aural input in the target language, their knowledge of the written language so far outstrips their ability to segment the oral language that segmentation seems even more formidable.

Video aids segmentation primarily through its multimedia nature. In a sense, segmentation is like cryptology. The most important step in breaking a code is always the first one. After that everything goes far more easily, not only because there is less code left to break, but also because a new logic has become available. In segmentation, this new logic is provided by the target-language message that the first break has begun to construct. Video's ability to provide correspondences between language and the real world makes this first breakthrough much more likely and much more rapid. Imagine a first-year student hearing another

Seeing a video of this woman gluing the handles to Limoges porcelain cups makes it much easier for students to recognize and retain the words for cup, handle, glue, and brush. (*La Porcelaine à Limoges*)

student's poor pronunciation of two German sentences: **Dasweissichnicht** and **Dasistnichtweiss** [I don't know; this isn't white]. Though hardly difficult, sentences like these can pose segmentation problems for first-year students. However, as part of a video clip showing a man shrugging his shoulders and a woman expressing surprise at her newly painted blue room, these expressions become much easier to segment and decode. In the same way, a second-year French student is less likely to confuse **pinceau** [brush] with **pain** [bread] and **seau** [bucket] in the context of a visible activity involving the use of a brush.

Video's diverse nature allows various solutions to the problem of segmentation. Some students will regularly segment by paying careful attention to the speaker's hesitations and pauses. Others will hear words for which they see objects in the background. Others will infer from the image a general context that permits them to predict the class of words that will probably be spoken. In the process, they will likely hear the words that actually are spoken. Still others will pay close attention to body language and similar discursive features. Some will even end up reading company names from the sides of trucks or the fronts of buildings shown in the video, thus turning one of the greatest impediments to understanding—unknown proper names—into a primary decoder. Indeed, this last approach to foreign language video viewing by some students can be generalized to good advantage by instructors with carefully prepared programs that furnish subtitles of any names or terms that might interfere with segmentation and thus comprehension.

The controllable nature of video provides still another possible approach to the difficult problem of segmentation. Since we know what is on the tape, and since we can usually figure out where the greatest problems lie, we can ask students to perform preliminary tasks that will serve as clues in the code-breaking process. Imagine, for example, that a video shows a skier with a difficult foreign-sounding name explaining why she is so thrilled to have won the downhill ski race. You know that her name itself may prove an impediment to many students, so you ask students in a preliminary exercise to answer questions about a table of sports results that includes the times, places, and overall classifications of the top downhill skiers. By the time they see the video, students have a headstart on the code. Familiar with the vocabulary likely to be used, as well as with the names of the major competitors, they can much more easily segment the sound track.

Syntax

Can video actually be used to teach grammar? Grammar has been taught out of context for so many years that it is easy to forget why it exists at all: in order to communicate, in order to make useful, recognizable distinctions. Not all grammatical distinctions are readily demonstrated through video's characteristic connections, but it is surprising how many of them are. Such familiar elements as personal pronouns, demonstrative adjectives and pronouns, reflexive verbs, the conditional, the past tense, and many others come alive when they are used to describe or manipulate real situations. Take the typical problem, common to numerous languages, of past tense usage. Which tense corresponds to what type of action? In the past, too many exercises on the imperfect/preterit distinction turned out to be only more or less disguised translation exercises. In keeping with a recent trend toward contextualized comprehension questions, video easily provides the necessary temporal context for handling tense and modal distinctions.

Another important contribution of video in the syntactic realm is the ability to distinguish between high-frequency structures and less important ones. Students usually find all grammar points printed in the same type. All rules, it seems, have the same value. Video programs belie such an egalitarian approach to grammar. With a regular dose of video materials, grammar time can be apportioned not according to the difficulty of the concept but according to the frequency of its use. Video can also exemplify to students how often authentic language ignores prescriptive grammar rules. Accuracy is surely an important goal in the overall framework of language teaching, but at this point the language-teaching profession is more in need of materials that demonstrate the possibility of effective communication with imperfect grammar than the well-known possibility of correct grammar with imperfect communication.

Semantics

Video's versatile image/sound connection offers innumerable opportunities for helping students to understand the semantic value of words, expressions, constructions, and even voice tone or body language. The most obvious of these opportunities involve the one-to-one noun, verb, or descriptive adjective correspondences that prove so helpful to students in the early years of language study. Even this seemingly simple correspondence goes beyond the neat relationships embodied in most textbook line drawings. As helpful as those drawings are, and as superior to first-language translations, they necessarily pare down words to their lowest common denominators. What a difference exists between a list of items used at the meal table accompanied by appropriate sketches and ten minutes of a film such as *Un Village se met à table,* in which students see an entire Norman village eat its way through the day.[6] Once students have seen that film, they know what a **bol** looks like and when it is used. They know that in many French families **assiette** refers to colored, transparent glass soup plates, used throughout the meal. They know that French knives and forks are bigger than ours, that the French set the table differently, that they often drink wine or cider out of what we think of as water glasses, and so forth. Ask a student who has seen this film to tell you what mental images a particular tableware term conjures up, and the examples proffered will no longer be watered-down American equivalents. Show this kind of video once, and your students will begin to substitute real-life target-culture examples for their American assumptions. If students view programs like this one on a weekly basis over four years of language instruction, the authentic visual dictionary formed in their minds will have grown significantly.

Two principles operate here. One is that of *variety*. For the sake of instructors' convenience, target-language vocabulary is often stripped of all its rough edges. Only the most common uses are presented, just

Video is an ideal way of conveying the nuances of culturally-specific terms such as **bol,** the lotus-shaped bowl from which the French drink their breakfast beverages. (*Un Village se met à table*)

as travel folders usually stick to certain familiar stock shots of famous cathedrals. When students escape from the protection of the classroom, however, they invariably find that the language is not quite so simple. One reason Americans rarely develop linguistic competence past a certain level is that the input they are offered does not surpass a certain level. Simplifying for the neophyte is fine, but if later materials fail to provide grist for the motivated student's mill, then no further progress will be possible.

By respecting variety we fulfill a second principle and learn a great deal about *semantic extent*. What does a window look like in Mediterranean countries? Look at a single drawing and you will learn little about the Mediterranean mental picture of a window. Watch a video program from any Mediterranean country and note the correspondence between

Even such basic terms as "bread" and "bakery" gain meaning from the contextualization provided by video, as in this scene of a French bakery truck delivering bread to a town without a bakery. (*Un Village se met à table*)

picture and sound. The semantic extent of the local term for transparent wall openings is quite different from that of the English—or, rather, American—word *window*. References to what we Americans call car windows, train windows, or envelope windows are bound to teach a further lesson about comparative semantic extent. Continual exposure to video's multimedia resources, with their ability to place the process of signification in the foreground, will provide students with a surprising amount of cultural information that they will not realize they have learned (much as students do not realize how much cultural knowledge they have about this country until they go abroad).

Systems of Discourse

In real life, our most effective contextualizing, that is, predicting of future messages on the basis of a recognized or posited context, is decidedly discursive in nature. Discursive contextualization involves recognition of who or what type of person is speaking, under what circumstances the speaking is being done, and what category of discursive strategy, form, or genre is being used.

> "Is that my colleague so-and-so about to speak up in the faculty meeting? He'll probably go into his song-and-dance about the lack of a faculty club again . . ."

> "Did you hear a siren? Oh–oh! With that new speed limit I know just what he'll say . . ."

> "Say, it's Johnny Carson. I love the way he . . ."

We know more or less what everybody is likely to say, especially if we know who the actors are and what the circumstances are. The same goes for various kinds of speech or forms of address. In a bar or at a ball game we do not expect to hear the same language as in a courtroom or at a fancy restaurant. The language of a love letter is different from the language of a traffic citation or a graduation speech. Discursive information provides an important shortcut to understanding. If this is true in a first language, it is all the more true in a second language. Yet textbooks rarely provide any information about the discursive context. Even when exercises are not discrete and independent, they rarely include discursive information for the benefit of the student. With video, discursive contextualization is everywhere present. We watch people speak, we see to whom they are speaking, we note the circumstances underlying their speech, and perhaps most importantly, we remark that the meaning of a word can change according to the discursive context. We also note that the same person may change language styles when moving from one discursive situation to another. The rapid-fire variety of discursive situations presented by video programs is certain to increase our awareness of the importance of discursive contextualization for ensuring comprehension.

Systems of Culture

When the French say **fenêtre,** it has been suggested, they do not see the same mental image as Americans see when they say *window.* "Culture is simply the sum total of all such differences within the language," affirms Barry Lydgate, co-creator of the video course *French in Action* and professor of French at Wellesley College. This elegant formula has the immense value of demonstrating just how closely language is tied to culture. With the building blocks of the one, the other must be built as well. In an important sense, then, all the comments previously made about semantic contextualization apply here. It is not possible to reach a clear understanding of the semantic extent of a given term without also reaching some understanding of the culture supporting the semantics. The same is true of syntax and systems of discourse. Anything that helps us to understand the language and its circumstances by definition contributes to our understanding of the culture.

The amount of information carried by video makes it an especially rich cultural vehicle. The label on a videotape may say it is a murder mystery or an educational program, but a careful observer notes much more: the shops and shopping patterns, the methods of locomotion, the signs and posters, the clothing, the eating habits, and so forth. The inhabitant of the culture takes these for granted, but for the foreign language learner, video's images and sounds become an open book made up of chapter upon chapter of cultural information. Even the video programs themselves—their construction, scripting, and cinematography—provide special insight into a nation's cultural specificity.

Video reminds us just how heavily we have concentrated on the written language to the near exclusion of authentic oral discourse and on teaching grammar and vocabulary rather than on providing comprehensible input. Video sets the standards and provides the methods for assuring a stable supply of comprehensible input. This chapter has sketched some of the theoretical assumptions underlying a video-based approach to the teaching of language and culture. The chapter that follows will address some of the more practical concerns of video pedagogy.

Notes

1. See especially Stephen D. Krashen, *Second Language Acquisition and Second Language Learning* (Oxford: Pergamon, 1981), and *Principles and Practice in Second Language Acquisition* (Oxford: Pergamon, 1982); Stephen D. Krashen and Tracy D. Terrell, *The Natural Approach: Language Acquisition in the Classroom* (Hayward, Calif.: Alemany/Janus Press, 1983); Tracy D. Terrell, Magdalena Andrade, Jeanne Egasse, and Elías Miguel Muñoz, *Dos Mundos: A Communicative Approach* (New York: Random House, 1986).

2. See Krashen, *Principles and Practice in Second Language Acquisition,* p. 141. The studies cited include James J. Asher, "The Strategy of the Total Physical Response: An Application to Learning Russian," *International Review of Applied Linguistics,* 3 (1965), 291–300; "The Learning Strategy of the Total Physical Response: A Review," *Modern Language Journal,* 50 (1966), 79–84; "The Total Physical Response Approach to Second Language Learning," *Modern Language Journal,* 53 (1969), 3–17; J. J. Asher and B. Price, "The Learning Strategy of the Total Physical Response: Some Age Differences," *Child Development,* 38 (1967), 1219–27; S. Kunihara and J. J. Asher, "The Strategy of the Total Physical Response: An Application to Learning Japanese," *International Review of Applied Linguistics,* 4 (1965), 277–89.

3. For a useful summary of the literature on this topic, see Alice C. Omaggio, *Teaching Language in Context: Proficiency-Oriented Instruction* (Boston: Heinle & Heinle, 1986), Chapter 3.

4. See, for example, John D. Bransford and Marcia K. Johnson, "Contextual Prerequisites for Understanding: Some Investigations of Comprehension and Recall," *Journal of Verbal Learning and Verbal Behavior,* 11 (1972), 717–26; Alice C. Omaggio, "Pictures and Second Language Comprehension: Do They Help?" *Foreign Language Annals,* 12 (1979), 107–16; Gunther A. Mueller, "Visual Contextual Cues and Listening Comprehension: An Experiment," *Modern Language Journal,* 64 (1980), 335–40.

5. See Thom Hudson, "The Effects of Induced Schemata on the 'Short Circuit' in L2 Reading: Non-Decoding Factors in L2 Reading Performance," *Language Learning,* 32 (1982), 1–31.

6. Distribution information on video programs mentioned in the text is contained in Appendix II, which begins on page 175.

CHAPTER 2
An Integrated Approach to Video Pedagogy

What is video? Is it a new technology, a simpler way of doing the old things, a film strip and sound recording in a single package, a feature film in a smaller slipcase? Is video a technique to be added to the teacher's arsenal, like pattern drills and Cloze exercises? Or is it a philosophy, an implicit statement about which parts of the educational process deserve to be privileged?

No doubt it is all of these, and more. If we are to discover video's full potential, however, we will have to break out of familiar molds and learn to see in video new opportunities and new solutions, rather than just a continuation of familiar patterns modified by a new technology or a new technique. To begin, we need to recognize some of the pitfalls that beset new users of video and some of the road blocks to a new and educationally justified video pedagogy.

For many years, as a member of both a French department and a department of communications studies, I have followed with particular attention the many reports on the use of films to teach language.[1] Although many of these approaches have been innovative, they seem to illustrate examples of what the new video pedagogy should not be. It will therefore be useful to review a few of the common practices that make feature films and their role in language teaching a poor model for the teaching of language and culture through video materials.

From 16mm to 1/2″

Until the era of the videocassette recorder, films were often used according to a schedule determined not by the language instructor but by the campus film society or a local theater. Based on the reasonable assumption that chances to hear the target language spoken are all too rare, instructors assigned students to view a film along with other spectators more interested in the film's entertainment value. Typically, students were prepared for viewing by a short lecture on the importance of cinema in the foreign culture; some information on the director, actors, and topic; and perhaps some vocabulary sheets with translations of difficult terms following their order of appearance in the film. Follow-up activities included a class discussion on the day following projection and/or a written review or essay on some aspect of the film.

Use of campus film projections presented the following drawbacks:

1. **Choice.** Rarely did the instructor have a chance to choose a specific film.

2. **Scheduling.** When a good film showed up, it was assigned, often regardless of the timing. Students from multiple levels were frequently sent to view the same film.

3. **Version.** Only in extremely rare instances did students have access to an unsubtitled version of the film.

4. **Control.** Language students sharing a showing with other viewers could not stop the film to clarify meaning.

5. **Length.** Because most available films were feature length, students were expected to pay close attention to one hundred minutes of uncontrolled, complex oral language.

6. **Comprehension.** Typically, students at lower levels came away with an overwhelming sense of inadequacy.

7. **Preparation.** Teachers rarely had sufficient prior access to the film to permit preparation of adequate materials. Traditional vocabulary lists kept students' eyes glued to their papers while impeding a direct experience of the film's aural aspect.

8. **Follow-up.** Lack of access to the film made it difficult to discuss scenes in any detail. Even when the film was available for classroom use, the need to manipulate a 16mm projector while teaching the class created major problems.

9. **Access.** Films in the 16mm format are expensive to rent and even more expensive to purchase.

10. **Overall effect.** These shortcomings often led students to consider films as supplements to the *real* work of the course.

At its best, the video medium opens new horizons for educators, solving many of the problems familiar to users of 16mm films.

1. **Choice.** Virtually all feature films once available on 16mm in the United States are now available on cassette, along with a growing number of programs from foreign television networks and educational TV producers, as well as domestic materials.

2. **Scheduling.** Teachers using purchased cassettes can make their own decisions about the scheduling of individual programs.

3. **Version.** Many programs, especially those that did not begin as films, can be purchased without subtitles. For those programs only available with subtitles, the subtitles are more easily covered on a television screen than on a cinema screen.

4. **Control.** With purchased cassettes used on a videocassette recorder, teachers have virtually absolute control over what programs to use and how to use them.

5. **Length.** Whereas feature films run approximately a hundred minutes, the programs available on videocassette vary from a couple of minutes to over an hour. Instructors also may vary the length of longer programs by breaking them up into smaller segments. An increasing number of programs are suited to short in-class viewing sessions.

6. **Comprehension.** Whereas feature films are nearly uniform in their linguistic difficulty, video programs vary widely in linguistic level, from very difficult to rudimentary.

7. **Preparation.** Easy access to video programs, including the ability to work with the cassette at home, means the ability to produce better preparatory materials. An increasing number of distributors of video progams include some preparatory materials with many of their tapes.[2]

8. **Follow-up.** Because videos can be used at will during class time or through independent language laboratory study, they lend themselves readily to programmed use throughout the semester. Furthermore, video materials can easily be viewed independently by absent students. Video is thus assured a presence at the center of the curriculum, rather than being relegated to a supplementary position as a cultural enrichment.

9. **Access.** On average, videocassettes can be purchased for under a hundred dollars; rental costs for recent 16mm films are at least the same amount.

10. **Overall effect.** Careful choice, preparation, and follow-up by the teacher all but preclude the possibility that video material will produce feelings of inadequacy in students. Potential linguistic and cultural gains, as well as ease of use, are thus maximized.

To teachers who have used feature films to teach language and culture, the potential solutions provided by video programs are apparent, especially with the wide variety of currently available video programs and preparatory materials.

From Enrichment to Integration

The instructor without a clear notion of how to make use of video's special qualities may inadvertently recreate many of the problems typical of feature film use. Most previous writing on video pedagogy has concentrated on appropriate classroom activities for use with a particular type of material and at a particular point in the course.[3] The approach championed throughout this book is radically different. The *integrated approach to video pedagogy,* as I will term the method outlined here, calls for video materials to be chosen and sequenced with careful attention to a student's global language-learning program. Classroom activities are thus but a small part of the video-oriented syllabus. Integrating video materials into the curriculum means concerted, programwide decisions regarding the amount, type, and location of video programs to be used. Successful integration requires sufficient forethought to assure maximum return from video-supported units.

For the individual teacher, the integrated approach calls for reasoned and interdependent decisions regarding (a) goals to be accomplished through the use of video programming, (b) choice of programs to be used, (c) location within the course, (d) preparatory activities, (e) in-class use of each program, and (f) follow-up activities.

Goals to Be Accomplished Through the Use of Video Programming

When *Jules and Jim* at the Bijou was the only show in town, the goal was simple: More target-language input is better than less target-language input; send students to see the film. With access to the VCR and a wide variety of purchasable programs, instructors no longer need to be governed by such simplistic goals. *With video we can control the input and its use.* The old rule of maximizing input is no longer sufficient. Which input needs to be maximized? Why? When? How? Nor is the notion of enrichment by itself sufficient. Which part of the learning process are we enriching? And if video is so good as an enrichment medium, why not make it central to the curriculum?

The integrated approach suggests that video materials should be primarily used not as dispensable add-ons but as a fundamental part of the course structure. Although first-time video users should not hesitate to try video whenever they have located an appropriate program, the best time to consider introducing video into the curriculum is long *before* the beginning of the semester, when textbook decisions are being made and before a class-by-class syllabus has been determined. Appropriate planning is not just a matter of practicality, involving the purchase of necessary video programs and advance reservation of videocassette recorders and lab space or other properly equipped rooms. Appropriate planning is also essential to the theoretical grounding of each part of the course. When instructors know *why* they are using a particular video, text, reading selection, or testing device, they have a much better chance of controlling it. Video is a powerful medium; but, like fire, it can do damage if it gets out of control.

Choice of Programs to be Used

A good rule of thumb is to assume that students can handle video selections no longer than three to six minutes for each college semester or secondary-school year of language study. As important as the amount of material is the careful selection of programs or sequences. What kind of logic should prevail in the selection of video materials for an integrated approach? One principle must be emphasized from the outset: if video is to be used in support of language or culture teaching, materials must be chosen *not for their inherent artistic value* but for their ability to fulfill a particular function in a particular course. Although artistic value should be of concern, its place should be appropriately subordinate. We are not choosing films for an Oscar or television shows for an Emmy; we are selecting educational tools. Choosing programs that are capable of carrying out well-defined tasks leads to successfully integrated courses.[4]

Location Within the Course

When feature films were used as a major language-teaching device, the other activities of the course were often interrupted for weeks at a time while attention was directed to understanding a film. With video comes a new liberty that enables the instructor to use the audiovisual material where needed, in terms of both time (week of the semester and day of the week) and space (in class, individually out of class, or in a group out of class). Since video selections often run only a few minutes, they can be placed anywhere within the course. A segment that is especially good for exemplifying use of different past tenses can easily be scheduled for language lab viewing or in-class attention even on days when other activities are expected to take up time. Some programs may be viewed out of class only, with classroom time devoted to follow-up work that requires the instructor or group. Other video sequences may be used in class without any overt preparation. Still others may be extended over many weeks and accompanied by a wide variety of preparatory exercises, in-class activities, and testing assignments.

Old habits die hard, to be sure, so we must fight to release ourselves from the hold of familiar feature-film practices. We must try to think of video as one of a group of basic techniques available for all sorts of teaching.

Preparatory Activities

The number and variety of preparatory activities that can be devised constitute the hallmark of the integrated approach to video use. However, video programs do have potential drawbacks that are compounded by the diversity of students in any given class. In order to be maximally useful, video programs must be both within and just beyond the reach of each individual student. The programs must be sufficiently under-standable to reinforce learning and produce a positive effect and yet must also always challenge the student to reach a little bit farther, to understand what could not have been understood the day before. Full comprehension of audiovisual programs makes special demands of students. Students cannot rely on standardized pronunciation, do not have the crutch of the written word, and cannot work at their own pace if the video is used in class only. The medium's audiovisual redundancy, it is true, often helps to promote the necessary understanding, even where the entire audio track is not fully understood. However, since our goal is to teach students to understand messages even with only minimal context, we cannot encourage students to rely totally on heavily con-textualized sequences.

Comprehension, then, cannot be taken for granted. In order for video programs to have maximum positive effect, students must be prepared for viewing. Usually, this involves providing a context for the program to be viewed, but not the kind of synopsis found in a television program guide nor the familiar list of difficult vocabulary. Integrating video into the curriculum means setting appropriate oral and written tasks for students in the days or weeks preceding a particular video segment, tasks that will give them the *general* background necessary for comprehension. Students may believe that their efforts are directed solely at understanding the assigned task. When the video comes along, however, they will transfer to the aural medium the knowledge gained in the written context. The video will thus serve to reinforce the printed text, while the printed text will constitute an appropriate introduction to and preparation for the video.

The number and type of preparatory exercises that can help students to make better use of video time are limitless. The following chapters will describe many such exercises and suggest when, how, and under what circumstances they might be used. For the time being, suffice it to say that teachers who use video must become magicians of a sort.

Without ever appearing to prepare students for a given video segment, they must give the students all the semantic, syntactic, and cultural background needed to transform the coming video program into an old friend instead of remaining a novelty. Recognition must be the keyword, so that students at all levels may receive positive reinforcement. Only with the comfort of recognition will most students accept the challenge of the unknown. With well-chosen preparatory activities, the video program can become as intriguing as a carefully constructed detective novel, with just enough recognition of the known to carry students forward in their search for new understanding of the unknown.

In-Class Use of Each Program

Teachers brought up on the Audiolingual Method often have a hard time avoiding pattern drills. However, a day-in, day-out routine of what are at first invigorating substitution exercises soon becomes a monotonous singsong. Video supporters should take this example to heart. As novel as video is in today's classroom, it will not always be so. The future of video as an effective teaching tool depends on our finding and implementing appropriate methods for each program. Video is not really a tool; it is a tool box. To each need corresponds a different tool, a different video approach. The biggest danger faced by new users of video is the enticement of a particular aspect of the medium, along with the temptation to concentrate on that same aspect again and again, to the exclusion of others. Perhaps this book and others like it will help individual instructors to vary their uses of video.

It is important to remember that classroom time is privileged time. Only in the classroom are students and teacher together. In many schools and colleges, class time is also the only time when group activities are possible. It is obviously *not* the time for lengthy bouts of video viewing. Class time should be used instead for fostering the productive skills. The obvious question—"What can I do with this video?"—should become "How can this video make class time productive? How can class time make this video more productive?" At first it is not easy to assess how much of a video program students are actually understanding. Classroom use of video gives an ideal opportunity to find out just what students understand. (*See Chapters 3 through 7 for specific examples of creative classroom activities.*)

Follow-up Activities

Full integration of video programs means more than just careful preparation and intelligent face-to-face use. It also means continued exploitation throughout the course. The video medium provides authentic examples of individuals speaking and acting. As such it automatically gives numerous opportunities for students to speak and act. Rare is the live television program (news, weather, game show, or the like) that does not inspire an appropriate model for student language production. (*See Chapter 4 for examples of appropriate activities for use with a weather forecast.*) Interview-based documentaries furnish all the necessary vocabulary for interview activities. Even a simple greeting may be seen as an opportunity to lead students from passive consumption of the video program to active language production based on the program.

Testing of various sorts constitutes a special case of follow-up language production. One of the most important problems to be resolved by instructors who use film or television materials is diminished interest on the part of students. As soon as students figure out that there will be no testing on a particular activity, they tend to become inattentive. Some informality is good, to be sure; it is important to give students some experiences early in the semester in which the sword of testing is not held over their heads. If the sword is spared too long, however, video may never be anything more than enrichment. When video is an integral component in a course, appropriate ways must be devised to test on and with video. These need not be complicated or difficult. Students love to witness their own progress, and carefully constructed testing devices can actually have a positive effect on student self-esteem. (*See especially Chapter 4.*)

The six aspects of the video integration process identified here do not begin to cover every single decision that instructors must make in order to develop a satisfactory program. However, they do provide an outline of appropriate standards and goals that should be met for the full integration of video materials into the curriculum.

From the point of view of the language coordinator or other person responsible for the overall "fit" of departmental offerings, still another concern must be addressed. Suppose that last year the third-semester class used televised weather reports with good effect, so this year the first-year course built them into a revised weather vocabulary unit, including geography and numbers under one hundred. What will happen next year, when this year's first-year students run into tapes in the third-semester class that they have already seen? If video materials are treated not as something extra that makes a program look more attractive but as an integral part of the basic foreign language education process, then such concerns will be taken care of. The best learning will take place in programs where an integrated approach to the use of video materials complements an integrated approach to the overall process of language learning.

Notes

1. For a representative sample of approaches to teaching language through cinema, see Geneviève Jacquinot, *Image et pédagogie: Analyse sémiologique du film à intention didactique* (Paris: Presses Universitaires de France, 1977); Richard Blakely, *Filmodules* (Rumford, R.I.: Professional Language Associates, 1981); Henry A. Garrity, *Film in the French Classroom* (Cambridge, Mass.: Polyglot, 1987).

2. Among available programs distributed with preparatory materials are Middlebury's *La Télé des Français,* Houghton Mifflin's Spanish and German programs, Heath's *97 Publicités télévisées: Le français en réclame,* and numerous PICS programs in French and German.

3. See, for example, most of the articles in the 1985 special issue of *Studies in Language Learning* devoted to video and second language learning (volume 5, number 1), as well as the items in the bibliography by Berwald, Buehler, Knight, Lancien, Lawrence, Lonergan, Santoni, and Silva.

4. See Chapter 11, Sources of Video Programming, for further suggestions regarding appropriate program choice.

CHAPTER 3

Basic Principles of Video Pedagogy

New teaching techniques and technologies have never been easy to implement. Berlitz and Sauveur had to develop a network of schools in order to put their Direct Method into practice. With the rise of the Audiolingual Method, thousands of language laboratories were built and equipped, and courses were widely restructured and rescheduled to take advantage of these newly available resources. What of video? Will it require similar investment and change in order to make a significant impact on educational practices? Can video materials be successfully integrated into existing courses without massive transformations of syllabi and resources? These questions deserve careful consideration. For many, they represent the major obstacles to a broad adoption of video programs in courses at all levels. This chapter directly confronts these commonly asked questions before moving on to consider other fundamental concerns for video pedagogy.

Finding Time for Video

"My syllabus is crowded enough as it is. How can I find time for video?" When instructors sit down to construct a syllabus they generally think in terms of independent units, each taking a more or less fixed number of class periods. This kind of thinking is especially visible at course revision time. "Let's give *Argent de poche* an extra day this year." "I think we can get *Le Rendez-vous* done in one less day." "We've got to find one more day for relative pronouns." Typically, part of the course is given over to grammar topics, grouped according to the chapters of the adopted textbook, with each chapter considered to require a particular number of class periods. Additional space is reserved for reading selections, and these are sometimes replaced by feature films or other texts, each of which is thought of as occupying a block of so many class periods. The art of constructing a syllabus usually involves distributing the grammar chapters throughout the year, assessing the appropriate points at which to abandon grammar for reading or other "variety" units, then fitting all units into the calendar of a particular semester or year, with special attention to holidays, midterm grade deadlines, and other important fixed dates.

When most people think of video, they immediately associate it with familiar "variety" units that combine reading and cultural enrichment. There is, of course, good reason for this. Increasingly used to replace reading selections, feature films seem to offer an appropriate model for the integration of video into language courses. If a Fritz Lang film is an appropriate replacement for a Heinrich Böll novel in a second-year German course, why not insert a video version of a Thomas Mann story into the same spot in the course? Two nearly antithetical responses are required to answer this question adequately. First, and most obviously, video programs *can* be used to great advantage as separate aural/cultural units, according to the model developed for feature films. Because videos simultaneously provide commentary on a culture *and* a fascinating example of that culture, well-chosen video programs often deserve to constitute separate course units.

However, this is by no means the only status available to video. Besides filling a role as a possible object of study, video can also constitute a *manner of study*—that is, a *technique* rather than a text. Seen from this point of view, video need not occupy independent units but may instead serve as the approach through which a given point is made, a given subject or skill taught.

In a teaching methods course, the areas of lecturing, pattern drills, and computer-assisted instruction might well be considered individual topics, each constituting a separate unit and receiving a well-defined number of class periods. In a language class, however, these same topics become techniques, methods of putting across a particular type of material. Any given unit might appropriately include a lecture, a pattern drill, and CAI work. It is in this incarnation—as a technique rather than a topic— that video is bound to have its greatest impact. And it is by approaching video from this perspective that the instructor will most easily find room for it in a traditional course.

For grammar or vocabulary lessons, it is useful to think of video as serving one of three different purposes: recognition, manipulation, or production.

Recognition

Take *any* new grammar point and select *any* video segment. Play the latter and ask students to recognize the former ("Raise your hand when you hear a relative pronoun"). This is an extremely appropriate exercise for grammatical categories of the most varied nature. It remains properly introductory because it stresses recognition rather than manipulation or production, but it encourages students to encounter and recognize the targeted form within authentic speech—that is, in the context in which it is actually used. An exercise of this type might take as little as five minutes in the middle of a class session devoted to a particular grammatical form. With planning, an instructor could reserve this technique for vocabulary or grammar where aural differentiation is crucial (as with personal pronouns, past tenses, numbers, and the like). Note that this kind of exercise can go anywhere in the curriculum, not only maximizing recognition of the particular grammar point or vocabulary item but also encouraging students to think aurally—to hear, as well as see, the targeted form.

Manipulation

Whether in language study or in other parts of the educational process, one of the most important aspects of any unit is the process of structured manipulation. The Audiolingual Method best exemplifies this process, since it is built on the assumption that structured manipulation leads directly to language acquisition. A principle is introduced and sufficiently described or exemplified for students to recognize the form in question. Students are then led through a series of drills in which they practice the principle. This structured manipulation helps them to internalize the principles involved and thus serves as an essential step in their progress toward independent production.

With grammar instruction, video's contribution to manipulation will depend heavily on the assumptions that the instructor makes about language learning. Let us consider relative pronouns, for example. A grammar-translation adherent might ask questions about the antecedent of relative pronouns identified in a video selection, as well as the case of the pronouns. A proponent of the Audiolingual Method will already have located the relative pronouns in the video segment and developed transformational exercises designed to foster controlled use of the structures. A follower of Krashen and Terrell's Natural Approach might simply ask numerous questions about the sequence just viewed, with the sure knowledge that this additional input, dependent as it is on comprehension of the targeted structure, will contribute to student language acquisition. With surprisingly little preparation and little more time than traditional classroom exercises, video can become a familiar method for contextualizing grammar and vocabulary by rendering them both authentic and audible.

Note that authentic video helps to lessen the problem of frequency of use so common in written texts. If you have a hard time finding something on German video, then chances are your students won't run across it much in Germany.

Production

Not surprisingly, actual production using the targeted forms or vocabulary is the most difficult goal to achieve in language courses. Even here, however, the creative use of short video passages can be most helpful. The use of past tenses, for example, varies sufficiently from language to language to give students problems. The most important differences appear only in extended narrations that successfully set up multiple time levels. Successful production of extended narrations, however, is very difficult to attain, even at the intermediate level. Video is especially good at providing the necessary narrative context for distinction among past tenses. Imagine a short video narrative long enough to establish time levels, supported by a series of questions calling for a response in the past perfect:

1. Why was Maria crying in the opening scene?
   [She had learned that her husband was going to die.]
2. When had he found out that he had cancer?
   [He had discovered he had cancer in August 1973.]
3. Before the amputation what had she done to ease his pain?
   [She had asked the nurse to give him morphine.]

Carefully worded questions, often using the targeted form, call on students to make appropriate decisions about the correct tense or term, as well as actually to produce that form. Depending on the instructor's pedagogical persuasions, improper but understandable tenses may be corrected, either by direct comment or the formulation of questions that make meaning depend on tense. In any case, the ease with which a well-chosen video passage can provide a temporal context for tense work will soon become evident to instructors who use the medium.

The key to finding time for video, then, lies in understanding video as a technique rather than as a topic and in using short video segments. Pattern drills are rarely used for more than ten consecutive minutes. Video can profitably be used in the same way. Spend six or eight minutes on recognition of a particular grammatical form in a particular video segment, then move on to some other approach, not necessarily involving video.

If you have VCRs in your language lab or another convenient campus facility, the problem of building video into the curriculum is of course simplified. Preliminary work can be done by students as part of their homework, making in-class video use more fruitful in less time. Even if no video lab is available, however, a great deal of economy can be derived from thoughtful use of homework assignments. Students can,

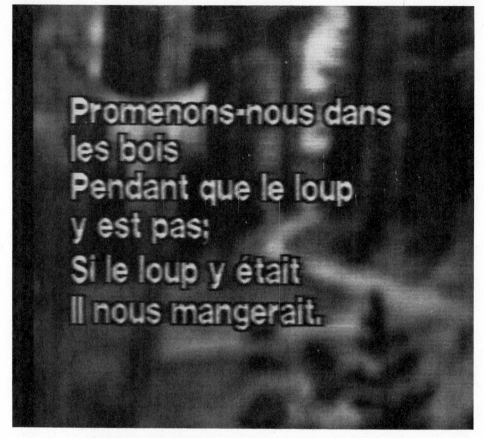

Promenons-nous dans
les bois
Pendant que le loup
y est pas;
Si le loup y était
Il nous mangerait.

Oral language production can be successfully fostered at the lower levels by video programs that provide lyrics for the music and invite students to sing along. (*Little Red Riding Hood,* Grimm version)

for example, be assigned a reading selection summarizing part of the video segment that is to be used in class the next day. Comprehension questions on this passage will familiarize students with the vocabulary and make it easier for them to follow the video segment and thus to locate the grammatical forms on which the next day's lesson will concentrate.

Building Video In

Instructors may well ask, "If I am to use video as a technique as well as a topic, does this mean that I have to wheel a VCR and monitor into class every time I want to make use of video?" By no means. It is worthwhile to recall that a video program is made up of multiple aspects. Although we normally experience video as a unified phenomenon, we can easily isolate the separate categories of image, sound track, and written transcription. Any one of these aspects can be treated separately, hence the enormous versatility of video. Building video into the structure of a particular course or curriculum thus involves two different series of concerns: Where will the work be done? What aspect of the video material will the work concentrate on?

By and large, video-oriented work may be done in any of the three following basic situations: the classroom, the language laboratory, and student homework assignments.

The Classroom

Although the classroom is far from being the only place where video is effectively used, it remains the key location for teaching students how to get the most out of video. Before scheduling a video program for class time, I always ask myself, "Is this the only place where this kind of work can be done?" Class time is at a premium, and anything that can be done outside of class will leave more time for important face-to-face activities that can be carried out only in the classroom. For example, class time is not well spent defining vocabulary. Furthermore, uncontextualized vocabulary should not be the major means of introducing a video program. The night before showing a video, I often give students a reading selection to prepare, including the key vocabulary for the next day's video. When class begins, the most pertinent terms or expressions are reviewed in the context of the already familiar passage. In this way, students realize that language is not an affair of grammar lessons and vocabulary lists but a matter of meaning and communication. Class time is thus spent reinforcing understanding rather than introducing vocabulary.

In spite of popular assumptions, class time is best reserved as *the court of last resort* for video usage. In the integrated approach, decisions about video and other techniques alike are made in the context of broader educational concerns. The classroom will commonly be reserved for activities that require face-to-face contact: teacher evaluation of student understanding; exemplary activities showing students how to process video input and replicate it in lab or homework situations; recognition, manipulation, or production exercises necessarily initiated by the instructor; manipulation or production activities requiring group interaction; and testing devices not appropriately carried out without the presence of the instructor. Other activities surely deserve to be added to this list, but the principle will remain the same: avoid wasting valuable class time on work that can be done elsewhere.

The Language Laboratory

For language laboratories that are at present poorly equipped, numerous solutions are at hand. Video's audio side can easily be recorded on audiocassettes and used just like any other audiotape. By itself or in conjunction with handout materials (sketches or copies of video images, maps, checklists, questionnaires, and the like) or jealously guarded lab materials (slides, realia, and so on), audio copies of a video sound track can go a long way toward making an audio lab into a video support system. If you are using video at all, you must have some video equipment. Try using part of the lab or an adjacent classroom for video lab purposes. Given that other needs for the VCR and monitor may exist, this video lab may be available only a few hours a week, but unless your program is large, such a temporary arrangement may be sufficient.

Access to a video lab, however modest, facilitates video use of many types. Perhaps most important, it permits the instructor to increase students' exposure to contextualized authentic speech and to vary the types of exercise for students to prepare. In particular, the video lab makes it possible for individuals or small groups to work at their own speed, thus facilitating individualized instruction based on exercises in a video workbook. In a lab, students can talk to each other about the video program without the restraining presence of the teacher. In a lab, students can listen again if they have not understood or go on to the next passage rather than wait for the slower students to catch on. In a video lab, students can concentrate on exercises far more complex than those that can be handled either in class or without the contribution of the moving image. Video labs are too useful not to be made widely available.

Student Homework

An instructor may well ask, "If a student has not yet seen a given video program, how can that student possibly do video homework without a personal VCR?" Before too long, it may be possible to assign video projects for student preparation on home or dorm videocassette recorders. For the time being, however, more modest goals are in order. Video homework does not necessarily require the video. Even if it does not include video viewing, homework can contribute markedly to video pedagogy, whether through preparatory exercises and readings, analyses of photocopied video images or transcripts, and cultural commentaries or essays based on prior viewing, not to mention testing of various sorts. (*More concrete suggestions appear in Chapters 4 through 7.*)

These three situations, by the way, are not the only ones possible. A French House or German Club, a Tavola Italiana or Hispanic Hour, clearly offer opportunities for integrating video into the program in novel ways. Perhaps international television materials can be fed to the campus or community on a local-access channel, provided the necessary permission is obtained. Is there a foreign language lounge on campus or another location where international video can be viewed?

Thinking in terms of potential locations for video is especially helpful in developing a syllabus and trying to distribute work appropriately. In truth, however, a confident attitude is needed in order to generate the actual tasks, activities, and exercises necessary for day-to-day teaching. Another breakdown of possible ways in which to use video reveals the extent to which the educator's use of video differs from entertainment video. When we sit at home watching television, we absolutely insist that all aspects of the experience be available at all times: the picture must be clear and bright, the sound must not be muffled, the dialogue must be understandable. Curtail any aspect and the viewer will immediately start fiddling with the dials, trying desperately to return the video experience to its appropriate audiovisual unity. For the educator, on the other hand, the possibility of using less than the full audiovisual phenomenon—the image alone, the sound alone, the script alone, or none of the video at all—reveals some of video's most important educational benefits. When the VCR is conceived of as a combination of many different machines—that is, television, film strip or slide projector, and tape recorder—the teaching possibilities are innumerable. In thinking about the many video activities available, then, it may be helpful to consider a variety of approaches.

Image and Sound Together

To be sure, video's most fundamental quality is its ability to provide fully contextualized examples of authentic language. In order to assure access to this contextualization, the early years of language study of necessity depend heavily on simultaneous use of both channels of information. Even beginners, however, will gain markedly from a progressive weaning from the characteristic overdetermination of the audiovisual medium. Certainly, comprehension is enhanced when students can see the vegetables that a Spanish housewife displays one by one as she mentions their names. Early exercises based on programs with heavy image/sound redundancy may well use both image and sound. Later exercises, however, will quite appropriately break away from the mutual reinforcement of the audiovisual complex in order to encourage understanding of the uncontextualized sound track or foster language production inspired by the silent image. Just as classroom time must be jealously saved for activities requiring the teacher and class, so full audiovisual presentations of the video material should be made not as a matter of course but as the result of a reasoned decision, with all the alternatives considered.

The Image Alone

Although especially appropriate for teaching students to derive maximum cultural benefit from the image, use of the image by itself is also helpful for encouraging student comments and conversation. Often students who can tell you most about the image, and even about its particular cultural components, are the weakest students, the ones least likely to have understood the dialogue. There is a good reason for this. Understanding the language makes culture seem natural; once the language makes sense, everything else seems appropriate and obvious. Some aspects of culture require a full understanding of the language, but it is amazing how many cultural concerns become invisible by virtue of an understanding of the language itself. The student who is unable to understand the dialogue is thus often freed to pay closer attention to the image, just as we all do when we watch an unsubtitled film in an unfamiliar language.

How do you get students who are concentrating on the dialogue to notice a culture's conventions for salutation? How do you get spectators who are eager to follow the narrative to notice the laundry hanging from the windows or the billboards in the background? Turn the sound off. The eerie feeling that follows is perfect for teacher commentary, student response, and general sensitivity to the parts of culture directly carried by the image itself. The instructor can attract students' attention to the few items that cannot be recognized without the sound track. When the sound is turned back up, students will find themselves in an instructor-inspired cultural detective story. Pique their curiosity with the image alone, then use that curiosity to energize attention to the far more difficult sound track.

Working with the image alone can also serve to spur student language production. Never easy to assure, language production can often be helped along by the silent flow of images to be described, commented on, or otherwise accompanied. At early stages, language production may mean simply producing any word corresponding to the image. In a conversation course, it might mean responding to the teacher's questions as the tape rolls by. In an advanced language course, it could take the form of on-the-spot news commentary, with students treating the video image like a live news event. Using the image alone also permits the instructor to substitute a simpler or a special-interest commentary for the video's original sound track, either in person or by means of a recorded second sound track. Used with creativity and initiative, the

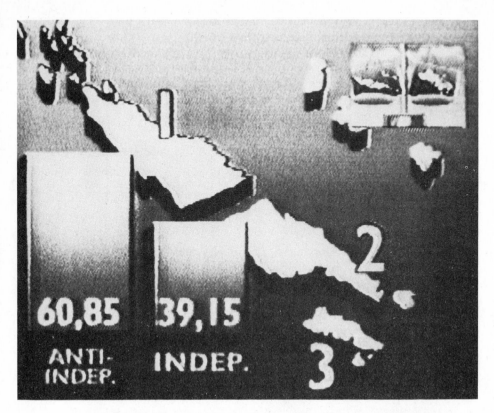

Video programs or news items with maps and graphics are especially suited to work without the sound track. Students who start by viewing this map of New Caledonia and its accompanying graph on the results of a vote on independence will more easily understand the news report as a whole. (*Télé-douzaine*)

image alone, with or without the implied connection to one sound track or another, provides endless possibilities for activity. Remember, though, that it does take equipment and effort to produce a *moving* image. If all that is required is commentary on a still image, then there may be a more economical way of producing that commentary than through the still-frame button on the VCR. There is no use pulling out the video cart if a picture from *Der Spiegel*, a Canadian newspaper, or a Mexican travel folder would have sufficed.

The Sound Alone

Video's greatest strength may be its ability to provide a visual context for sound, but sound retains many possibilities for independent use. The original sound track from the video program can easily be made available to students both in class and outside class. In class, the instructor's familiarity with the video monitor should permit convenient variation between video's normal audiovisual existence and either the image alone (simply by turning the sound off) or the sound alone (by turning all the way down either the brightness or the contrast, depending on the monitor). Alternation between sound alone and sound plus image provides multiple opportunities of the following types:

1. **Sound and Image Together, Then Sound Alone.** This is especially appropriate for freeing students from dependence on the visual context. Play a program through once, ask basic questions to assure general understanding, then play only the appropriate part of the sound track, preceded or followed by relevant questions.

2. **Sound Alone First, Then Sound and Image Together.** This technique, most appropriate for use with more advanced classes, challenges students to understand on the basis of sound alone. It invites students to guess what is going on in the image on the basis of the sound, an extremely fruitful combination of listening exercise, prediction, and oral production.

3. **Sound Alone First, Then Image Alone.** This technique is a variation on the preceding approach, with still greater emphasis on oral production. Have students listen to just the sound, then ask them to narrate the story or describe the events on the basis of the image alone. Their narrations can either alternate with the image or, for advanced classes, take place while the image is running. This approach works best with sequences that carry independent information on the sound track.

The video sound track can, of course, be separately recorded and exploited. Not only will audiocassettes permit you to use existing language laboratory facilities to extend video pedagogy opportunities, but in this era of portable audiocassette players, you may actually be able to fit *Rotkäppchen, El pueblo sumergido,* or *Télé-douzaine* into your students' daily jogging routine. This approach involves choosing programs with appropriate copyright clearance or seeking clearance yourself, but since it opens new vistas for video pedagogy, it is well worth pursuing. In the past, students have often been sent to the lab to do repetitive trans-formation exercises based on an all-too-limited and uncontextualized vocabulary. A better alternative is to develop interesting audio exercises based on a video sound track and alternate the exercises with the sound track on the same tape. One can imagine many uses for this kind of modified audio lab approach. For example, if a language lab cannot provide independent, drop-in video viewing, students might watch a program together in an adjacent classroom and then work with the sound track on audiocassette in the existing lab. This method easily extends available facilities and usefully complements class time.

If time permits, you may want to produce a second sound track for an appropriate program. The second sound track might provide a simplified commentary for lower-level students, but many other types of material could be included. For example, a sound track used to review a particular program might be limited to questions about the image. Another sound track might relate the criminal's version of a story originally narrated by the detective. A third might replicate the original script but leave out words, substitute synonyms, or use clearer pronunciation. Since all these things take time, they might best be accomplished by your doing an alternate sound track for one program while a colleague concentrates on another.. *(See Chapter 10 for practical information on recording an alternate sound track.)*

Neither Sound nor Image

Paradoxically, by far the majority of video-oriented activities take place in the absence of both sound and image. Preparatory work is commonly carried out far from a VCR. Exercises based on a video program seldom depend on a second viewing of the program. Even classroom activities often involve oral production based on the video material but developed in its absence. Written production likewise grows out of video viewing but rarely requires viewing facilities.

In a way, then, this mode presents a special challenge for the video-oriented teacher. The preceding chapter discussed the importance of integrating video materials fully into the curriculum by respecting both the potential of video and the educational mission that it serves in a particular course or situation. Decisions regarding video should be tailored to the educational situation at hand. However, the inverse is true as well. The course as a whole should be fitted to the video materials. We must be mindful of video's potential even when video is not immediately present in the course. Just as we think far ahead in a literature or civilization course and lay the groundwork today for a discussion that we know will come a month hence, so we can easily prepare students for the video to come by our choice of reading selections or grammar exercises. By the same token, we can take advantage of a previously viewed program by assigning tasks that require students to make use of the vocabulary, grammar, and cultural knowledge to which an earlier program exposed them.

This overview of the basic principles of video pedagogy does not provide many detailed suggestions. These will come in the following chapters, where approaches appropriate to particular skill levels and class types will be discussed. For the time being it should be enough to identify categories of use so as to help individual instructors get the most out of their video materials and vary their techniques.

The Golden Rule of Video Pedagogy

If this book could be reduced to one principle, it would surely be that of *integration*. Similarly, the Golden Rule of video pedagogy, a rule that should be remembered every day and every hour, would be: *Don't expect— or even seek—full comprehension*. As an illustration of this principle, listen to an authentic program from a country with whose language you are perfectly familiar. Although you understand the program, you may have trouble faithfully transcribing any segment of the tape. For example, although you know what the sentence means, you may not be really sure how to spell a name or two. This is how your most advanced students feel on their best days. Consider the experience of a beginner. Unless extremely simplified tapes specifically produced for beginning students are being used, a first-year class will be extremely disconcerted by their first experiences with video, just as they would be by their first experiences abroad. They will have a hard time isolating words, let alone understanding sentences.

We must learn to become *tolerant of incomplete comprehension*. Even in our own native language we rarely follow every word of a TV news broadcast, every image of *Dallas,* every note of a Muzak recording. Modern media make up for our lack of complete attention by bombarding us again and again with basically the same information. We sometimes complain that television is pitched to the lowest common denominator. Let us take advantage of that fact by using foreign television to educate students who have not yet surpassed the lowest common denominator of any foreign country. In order to do that, we need to teach students how to profit from programs that they understand incompletely. By carefully evaluating the level of understanding to be expected from any given class and placing emphasis on that level of comprehension, we will eventually convince students that incomplete understanding is the norm and that their task is to achieve better rather than complete comprehension.

It is surprising just how easy it is to accomplish this. Consider a first-year class during the very first month. What video exercises can possibly be performed with beginners like this? Students might be asked to identify articles, numbers, personal pronouns, verbs in the present tense, or any items that they have thus far encountered in the video. This teaches students to hear, to break down the spoken chain into appropriate chunks; it gives students practice in understanding. *At the same time, it does not ask them to understand what they are not yet prepared to understand.* Their confidence is reinforced, their aural skills are being trained, and video's unique qualities are being exploited, but according to the level of the students in question.

At higher levels the same rules apply. Challenge the students to understand, but do not assume that understanding is a global, unified activity. Understanding happens in pieces; in pieces it must be taught. Accordingly, we need to help students to learn one piece, using video to reinforce that particular skill or item of knowledge, and then move on to another area. If we merely play the video and then question students for comprehension, we have become testers rather than teachers.

Two obvious corollaries of the Golden Rule of video pedagogy deserve mention here. First, it is essential that instructors remain at all times aware of their students' level of understanding. Instructors may be far more likely to overestimate student comprehension in the case of video than in the case of reading or conversation. It is hard, indeed, for teachers to remember that a student's major problem with any aural input is not so much comprehending as dividing continuous speech sounds into the appropriate words. For us, listening is like reading speech. For students it is usually more like finding the objects hidden in the drawings of trees. Check student comprehension early and often. Accustom students to taking in-class recognition or comprehension quizzes. When student understanding does not live up to your expectations, do not hesitate, especially in your first experiences using video, to modify your lesson plan or proposed approach.

A second corollary of the Golden Rule is to avoid asking students to accomplish direct transcriptions of the video sound track. Even in graduate courses on subtitling, experienced subtitlers and native speakers show constant difficulty with the transcription process. In a subtitling course some measure of transcription is necessary, but not many students should be expected to handle language at quite so advanced a level. When students transcribe a video program, they invariably spend too little time on important concerns and too much on the few truly difficult points. For example, instructors may realize that a given problem is caused by a faulty sound track, the use of slang, or an unusual regional expression, but students will waste far too much time if they are not forewarned about such problems. Even forewarned students may eventually be hindered by the erroneous notion that written accuracy is the only appropriate standard for video comprehension. To be sure, there are times when written accuracy is appropriate, especially when the instructor has weeded out the inaccessible passages by careful choice, partial transcriptions, or the use of the Cloze technique. Overall, however, teachers are far better served by targeting particular spheres than by insisting on complete comprehension.

In spite of familiar assumptions, students who have been exposed to the necessary vocabulary will not *ipso facto* understand a particular audiovisual program. Too much is involved in the learning of language and culture for a simple list to serve as a passkey. If it were that easy, then most of us would be without a job. Instead of assuming or expecting full comprehension, discover the liberating effect of partial understanding. We live with it daily in our own language. We can teach our students more about another language by helping them to recognize that their knowledge must grow little by little, topic by topic. We will be better teachers for it, and our students better—and happier—students.

PART II

Teaching with Video

CHAPTER 4
Video in Lower-Level Language Courses

In many ways, the lower-level language sequence is the key to successful video pedagogy. This is where the challenge is greatest and the rewards most meaningful. The choice of appropriate materials is most difficult at this level, but it is here that well-chosen materials will reach the largest number of students and remain in the curriculum for the longest time. Good video habits developed in the initial stages of language learning stay with students for years. By following a small number of simple principles, instructors can easily develop their own successful methods for using video in lower-level language courses. The first half of this chapter is thus devoted to a few basic guidelines of lower-level video pedagogy. The second half of the chapter suggests a broad variety of activities and exercises on which instructors might appropriately model their own.

Guideposts

Do Not Use Video Just to Use Video.

An appropriately integrated approach to video requires careful decisions about the function of video materials within the curriculum. If you cannot find the appropriate video program, abandon the idea, at least for now.

There is an obvious corollary to this principle: *start slowly, adding video one unit at a time*. It is more important to find a single well-chosen program, accompanied by a few well-conceived exercises, than to fill a course with whatever video materials happen to be in the local collection. Instead of buying ten programs for your first-year language sequence, buy the two that seem to meet your needs most clearly. Build them into the course this year, and then next year buy two more. This approach is far more realistic both for the departmental pocketbook and for your own time commitments.

Choose Materials Carefully.

Answers to the question "Why use video at all?" would surely mention its authenticity, its representation of real speech, its visual reinforcement, its presentation of the nonverbal aspects of language, its value as a cultural vehicle, and its motivating potential. Yet there is no guarantee that these qualities will be built into a particular foreign language video program. American-made programs often offer easy comprehension—but at the expense of authenticity. Documentaries typically maximize cultural benefits, but since they rely heavily on voice-over narration, they often fail to reveal the relationship between verbal speech and body language. The most eager class rapidly becomes discouraged when a difficult video program intensifies latent feelings of incompetence. There are hundreds of ways to choose the wrong program; it takes careful evaluation to discover an appropriate one. Constant consideration of two simple guidelines will invariably increase your chances of success.

1. **Have Clearly in Mind the Function You Expect the Program to Perform.** In identifying the expected function, you will not necessarily reduce video's multipurpose nature to a single aspect. You may very well have multiple functions in mind, but they should correspond to consciously formulated goals. To be sure, a video search need not always focus on one specific need. Many of the most exciting video discoveries will support a different part of the course from the one you set out to develop. The principle still holds, however, for the unexpected find, the program that will work perfectly for week three when you were looking for something to use in week eleven. Ask yourself what you will use the program for. Do you know why you are choosing it? Does it correspond to the teaching you want to be doing at that point in the course?

2. **Do Not Look for Long Selections.** The feature film is simply not the appropriate model here. In the first two years of foreign language study, three to ten minutes is an ideal length; anything over twenty minutes stretches both students' attention span and your crowded syllabus to the utmost.[1] It is not always necessary to present a complete program or story. If you find five perfect minutes in a thirty-minute documentary, use just the five minutes. If a twenty-six-minute narrative program that seems too long for you contains one scene that corresponds nicely to your needs, have the students read a summary of the first thirteen minutes, and then use your scene in class. Give the students the choice between reading a summary of the rest of the program and seeing the

last ten minutes in the lab. It is often better to choose three satisfactory minutes from a longer program than to assume, just because they are short and cute, that television advertisements will provide the perfect teaching tool. Often these ads use little language and rely heavily on slang, abbreviations, and cultural in-jokes or privileged references. Ads also hide unsuspected legal problems.[2] Like other programs, ads should be carefully chosen according to their linguistic and cultural potential. In particular, know what function you expect a specific ad to play at a given point in a given course.[3]

View a Video Program Repeatedly and Completely before Assigning It.

Thanks to responsible introductions on vocabulary and grammar range, along with our own experience in skimming printed material, we do not have to read every page of a new textbook to have a pretty good idea about its content and approach. Selection is more difficult when we use electronic media. Decades have been spent learning to scan and evaluate printed texts properly, but we are still in our infancy as regards video texts.

Unpleasant surprises will be avoided if *every* minute of every program assigned is carefully previewed. Important problems to be considered during previewing include identification of key cultural concerns, monitoring of vocabulary, and location of grammatical structures that can be used to good advantage, as well as structures not yet studied by the class. In addition, it makes good sense to determine which sequence or sequences will be used, to decide where they will best fit into the course, and to consider how their potential may best be tapped.

Actively Manipulate the Comprehensibility of All Video Programs.

Use every technique at your disposal to make sure that each video selection is at the appropriate level of difficulty for the students who will use it. This is especially important for first-year students. You can perform this sleight of hand by preparing either the tape or the students. Preparing the tape, a relatively new idea, is one of the great flexibilities offered by the video revolution. Whereas films, slides, and filmstrips, all products of an earlier chemical era, were fixed once and for all, video carries with it all the striking capacities of the electronic era. One of the first to recognize the importance of video's mutability was Jean-Pierre

Television commercials are often good springboards for lively conversation, such as this French life insurance ad, which is rich in interesting aural information as well as useful graphics and printed text. (*Télématin*)

Berwald, who over a decade ago began preaching the benefits of tampering with television materials. Since then, other educators, such as Louis Olivier have demonstrated the potential usefulness of modifying the image, sound track, or order of the original cassette.[4]

If your school has access to a character generator, commonly known as a CG, you can put subtitles in a program wherever you want. The term *subtitle* has been saddled with negative connotations because of the crude, truncated, and inaccurate translations that often accompany foreign films. Creatively used, however, subtitling is a promising pedagogical aid. Use subtitles as a source of information to make the program easier to understand by providing glosses for difficult vocabulary or unrecognizable acronyms (**CEE = Communauté Economique Européenne** [EEC], **DBP = Departamento de Bienestar Público** [Welfare], **DDR = Deutsche Demokratische Republik** [East Germany]). Subtitles also can be used to spell out unknown names mentioned on the sound track, to headline key figures mentioned only briefly by the announcer (**Familles avec télévision: 18% en 1961, 91% en 1984**), or to give information that will be the object of classroom exercises or discussion (weather data, phone numbers, sports scores, and the like). Use subtitles as well to ask questions about the current program in exercises covering grammar, vocabulary, or cultural concerns. Subtitles can be used even for testing. Because producing subtitles requires special equipment and a significant investment of time, many instructors will prefer to begin by trying out commercially available programs that make creative use of original language subtitles.

With a little imagination you and your VCR can also provide an alternate sound track that will serve many of the same purposes as subtitles. As mentioned in Chapter 3, you can replace the existing sound

Even without a character generator, teachers can make good use of linguistic texts that form part of a video program itself. This scrolling announcement shows the evening schedule of programs at the end of a *Télématin* broadcast.

track with another of your own invention—for example, a simpler version, an aural Cloze version lacking certain words, or a version with questions about the image. Assuming you have the appropriate copying rights, this alternate sound track can be put on a second copy of the original program, unless you have had the forethought to buy a sophisticated VCR that permits you to move back and forth from one sound track to the other on the same tape. (*More information on hardware choices may be found in Chapter 10.*)

The question of order will be much more easily handled once the videodisc player becomes more widely available. In many cases, it may be preferable to play a later scene before an earlier one, because the order of information, grammar, or vocabulary is better suited to class needs. Although the tape can be rewound in class, that solution is never a perfect one. Another solution is to dub the tape with the scenes in the desired order, but a copy made in this way takes time to prepare and may sacrifice quality of image. With a videodisc player, however, you can easily choose the order you want, with little loss of time and no loss of quality. This is clearly the solution of the future—and for some instructors actually is the solution of the present. One drawback to the use of videodiscs, however, is the current scarcity of international materials on videodisc.

Preparing the tape to manipulate its difficulty level involves a heavy investment in time and equipment. Preparing the students, on the other hand, requires only ingenuity and good sense. The basic theory underlying this approach might be expressed as follows. Because instructors are eager to provide a maximum dosage of understandable but challenging comprehensible input they regularly temper their own speech in such a way that students are likely to understand. Experienced teachers constantly read students' eyes to assess their comprehension level. When they sense that a word has not been understood or that a sentence is beyond the students' level, they try again through periphrasis, direct definition, a drawing on the blackboard, or, in extreme cases, a translation. Such continued interaction is, of course, not possible with video. The video text cannot conceivably revise itself constantly in order to match the needs of students with different backgrounds. By carefully choosing previewing activities, however, we can assure that the entire class has most of the knowledge necessary to understand the program at hand. Some preparation can be provided simply by intelligent choice of video material. Although the presence of a few unrecognized forms presents no problem, it clearly makes little sense to assign a retrospective doc-umentary to a class that has not yet studied any past tenses. However, when a first-year class is learning weather expressions and numbers up to one hundred, what could be more appropriate than a TV weather report or two? Authentic weather forecasters will use a few words that students will fail to recognize, but by matching student knowledge of

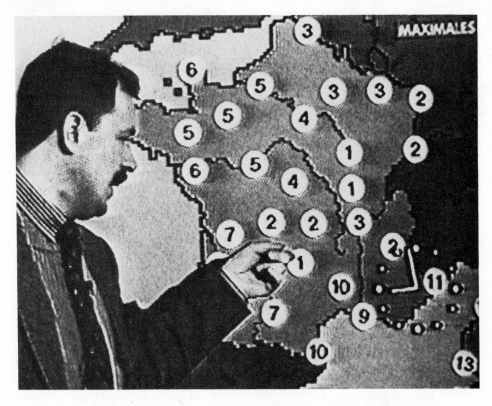

Weather maps are a good source of cultural and linguistic information and can be easily adapted for use at any level. (*Télématin*)

weather vocabulary and numbers to a program that uses that knowledge, we virtually guarantee a high level of comprehension.

Choice alone, however, is not enough. More active intervention is usually helpful and sometimes essential. Let us further analyze the example of the weather forecast, a good choice for the early weeks of the first year. In a typical forecast, the following problems may appear:

1. Temperatures expressed in Celsius degrees.
2. A few weather expressions not mentioned in the text.
3. A weather map not showing the spelling of the cities mentioned.
4. Some cities mentioned that are unfamiliar to the students.
5. Some unfamiliar names of regions, bodies of water, and countries.

On the positive side, the following opportunities are offered by the video and not explicit in the textbook:

1. An opportunity to provide a painless geography lesson.
2. A welcome chance to complement written expressions with more familiar oral equivalents.
3. A ready-made cultural lesson based on the Fahrenheit/-Celsius distinction.

The following previewing activities take into account the opportunities of this particular video along with its potential problems:

Provide a newspaper weather page, including a map of the country in question and a table of temperatures in various cities, given in both Fahrenheit and Celsius. A short prose forecast should follow, including unknown terminology from the video. Each of the following exercises based on this material might be carried out at home, in class, or both.

1. Simple number work ("What is the temperature in city *x*?").
2. More complex number work using the Fahrenheit/Celsius correspondence.
3. Geography work, concentrating either on names alone ("In what city is it *x* degrees?") or on the map itself ("In what city on the Rhine is it *x* degrees? Which city is closest to the Mediterranean?"). Among the cities targeted will be those featured on the video tape.
4. Work with vocabulary from the forecast that is not mentioned in the textbook. ("Where is a drizzle likely tomorrow? Where is it raining cats and dogs?"). This will help students recognize vocabulary on the video tape.

This type of preparatory work can be adjusted to suit any need. If you are studying time along with the lower numbers, you might add time zones. With a specially selected intensive class, you may want to include precipitation amounts with decimals. For a group on its way to Europe for a summer course, you might want to concentrate on the weather in the area where the course will take place. If your book provides an introduction to worldwide locations where the language in question is spoken, you may want two maps, one of a single country, the other of the entire world. Your geography questions might then be aimed at names of countries, continents, and oceans as well as cities.

Previewing exercises always aim simultaneously at two separate goals. While serving the needs of the course in general, previewing activities also prepare students to understand specific aspects of a particular video program. Let us take, for example, a typical news report on a downhill skiing race, taken from the morning show *Télématin*, broadcast by France's Antenne 2. Following is the transcript of that report:

En ski, ben, les Suisses dominent tout. Regardez cette demoiselle très acrobate—c'est la Suissesse Maria Walliser, qui a remporté hier la descente, malgré quelques petites fautes, devant une autre Suissesse, Michela Figini. Elle n'avait jamais de chance, Maria Walliser, et cette fois, eh bien, c'est fini; elle a remis les pendules à l'heure. Et elle était heureuse, heureuse, parce qu'elle n'avait jamais remporté de médaille d'or. Ecoutez, écoutez Maria Walliser, la charmante Maria:

"Pour moi, une médaille d'or ça compte pour ma vie, ça compte pour mon coeur, parce que je voulais avoir une fois un peu de chance, un peu plus de chance que j'ai eu aux autres Championnats du Monde et aux Jeux Olympiques."

Pas de chance pour la Britannique Claire Buff. . . . Plus de peur que de mal—elle a fait boum dans les matelas de mousse. On voit cette spectaculaire chute au ralenti. Une chute, mais enfin, sans bobo.

[In skiing, the Swiss women are winning everything. Look at this acrobatic young woman, the Swiss skier Maria Walliser, who, in spite of a few mistakes, finished first in yesterday's downhill race, ahead of another Swiss skier, Michela Figini. Maria Walliser had often been unlucky, but now her unlucky streak appears to be over. She was especially happy, because she had never won a gold medal. Listen to what the charming Maria has to say:

"For me, a gold medal counts for my life, it counts for my heart, because I wanted for once to have a little bit of luck, a little more than I had at the World Championships or at the Olympic Games."

No luck for the British skier Claire Buff. More alarm than harm when she ran into the foam-rubber mattresses. We see this spectacular fall in slow motion. A fall, but without an injury.]

This passage provides an ideal balance between the announcer's clear Parisian French and Maria Walliser's emotionally accented Swiss French.

Designed to be used with a unit on past tenses, this passage involves a number of minor vocabulary problems, as well as three difficult names to pronounce. How do you solve this problem for your students? The sequence is lively, motivating, well chosen for its grammar potential—in short, you want to use it. However, you are concerned that there may be some comprehension problems. A suggestion is to provide students with previewing exercises based on a mock newspaper article reporting World Cup results and standings. Such an article might look something like the following English version:

World Cup Results

March 22. At Val d'Isère yesterday, the Swiss skier Maria Walliser once again fell near the end of the course, surrendering her commanding lead to the young Italian sensation Maria Piccolina. Piccolina had already finished her second run, with a combined time of 2 minutes, 34.6 seconds, when Walliser started down the hill. Her first run had been so perfect that she finished in 1 minute, 15.5 seconds, nearly 2 seconds ahead of her nearest competitor. She was not so fortunate in her second run, however. Only three hundred meters before the end of the course Walliser lost her balance and fell. Piccolina thus won her second race of the season, followed by the Swiss skier Michela Figini in second place. The best French performance was registered by the future Olympian, Catherine Dumesnil, who finished fourth. Following are the World Cup standings before and after the March 21 race:

Old Standings	Points	New Standings	Points
1. Schenkel (Aut)	43	1. Piccolina (I)	48
2. Piccolina (I)	38	2. Figini (S)	44
3. Walliser (S)	37	3. Schenkel (Aut)	43
4. Figini (S)	36	4. Croton (S)	39
5. Croton (S)	35	5. Walliser (S)	37
6. Buff (GB)	34	6. Müller (RFA)	35
14. Dumesnil (F)	20	12. Dumesnil (F)	26

The article will familiarize students with some of the problem vocabulary and with all of the difficult names. It will also provide practice with past tenses, cardinal and ordinal numbers, and the names and abbreviations of European countries. The exercises based on the article might include questions like the following English equivalents:

Who won the downhill race on March 21?

Who was first after the first run?

What is her nationality?

Who was unlucky in the second half of the race?

Who was first in the general standings before the race?

What was her position after the race?

Who took over second place after the March 21 race?

Who was the only British woman in the top six before March 21?

By how many points does the best Frenchwoman trail the new leader?

Questions like these provide more than traditional comprehension checking, grammar review, and production practice. They also familiarize students with the vocabulary and proper names they are about to hear in the video, as well as the general standing of the people involved.

Preliminary work like this assures that students will carry the necessary information into their viewing session. Certain vocabulary terms are quite properly left aside, however. Important as it may be to guarantee basic understanding, students do need practice in learning from context, and providing such practice is certainly one of video's most important contributions to language decoding. For example, students can figure out the term **ralenti** [slow motion], used by the Antenne 2 announcer near the end of his report, with the help of semantic analysis (ra-**lent**-i) and the slow-motion photography that appears on the screen just before the term is pronounced. Similarly, the terms **matelas de mousse** [foam-rubber mattress] and **bobo** [child's word for injury] can easily be understood, the first from the video image and the second from the narrative context. Successful video pedagogy depends in part on careful dosage of appropriate proportions of preparation and contextual discovery. Consciously manipulating the comprehensibility level of a specific video program by no means implies abandoning the normal logic of your course organization. With ingenuity and foresight, you can maximize all of your returns.

Strive for Variety in Your Choice of Video Activities and Exercises by Using All Five Available Modes of Video Application, As Appropriate.

It is all too easy to get bogged down in the old familiar approach of dragging the VCR to class, along with a new videotape, every time interest seems to flag. This day-to-day approach has more than a few drawbacks, most of which can be avoided by the conscientious teacher who thinks ahead and keeps in mind the five fundamental video-oriented activities: preliminary exercises, activities for out-of-class viewing, in-class viewing strategies, review assignments, and video testing.

The best way to avoid repetition is to have some reference source, such as your own notes or this book, to serve as a constant reminder of the breadth of activities possible with video. For your students as well, this is a welcome guideline. The second half of this chapter provides a compendium of possible approaches.

Use Your Imagination and Your Good Sense.

To integrate video successfully into a lower-level language class requires an unusual combination of talents. Fortunately, the combination required is exactly the same as for any other teaching challenge. Without imagination, little will be accomplished; without good pedagogical sense, however, ingenuity alone will fail to produce the desired results. One eye must always be kept on the video and its potential, but the other eye must always focus on the course plan, on the general goals and methods set for this particular semester.

A short program entitled *D'hier à aujourd'hui: La population française* provides a particularly clear case in point. *D'hier à aujourd'hui* tells the story of several generations of a Breton family. The men are by and large followed around their work place or shown engaging in a characteristic activity, while the women spend most of their time talking together about their situation as women in modern France. Part of the film is thus perfect for lower-level use, because it provides maximum visual reinforcement and explanation of the sound track. The other parts, however, are too difficult to be used until later semesters. The best solution in a case like this is to split the film in two, using part of it at one level and, by prior agreement with a colleague, the other part at a higher level. Between the two of you, you might prepare identification cards for all of the major characters, with all the important information about them: identification number, date and place of birth, profession, address, phone number, and so on. Some of this information will be accurate and some necessarily fabricated. These "passports" may be used as the basis for preparatory exercises or, with appropriate blanks, may be filled in by students as they view the program. In class they can become the basis for activities of many types, with each student representing the character whose passport he or she holds. Support materials like these passports take time to prepare, but they unquestionably help you to integrate video materials more successfully into your curriculum.[5]

If active written or oral language production is your goal, do not hesitate to have students predict future events on the basis of a short clip from the program. Serving as a sort of "coming attractions" trailer, a well-chosen clip can whet students' appetite for more while enticing them to speculate on what will follow. On the basis of her research on schema theory, Alice Omaggio suggests that a similar exercise using a line drawing or a still from the video can significantly enhance student comprehension (and thus confidence, pleasure, and motivation).[6] This sort of exercise has the benefit of freeing you, if necessary, from the VCR. Ever-present schedule conflicts, remote classrooms, and unforeseen problems will surely make you welcome a method of continuing to work with the video material without actually having the tape at hand. Jean-Pierre Berwald suggests preparing a set of slides of key images, as well as an audiotape of the sound track, in order to maximize versatility and independence.[7] Although this technique may be too time-consuming for across-the-board application, it has many potential uses.

Be creative in combining tasks related to a single program. Do not assume, for example, that you have to play a tape to the end during class time. Whetting students' appetites with partial programs in class is a good way to get the most excited students to the lab to see more. Consider dividing a particularly attractive tape into multiple short sections and conducting the week's only in-class viewing at the start of class on Monday or Friday. Make-up viewings in the lab can be scheduled for those who missed the showing. Serialization worked in films like *The Perils of Pauline* and *Flash Gordon*. Why not try it with video on our own students? Another possibility is to hold back the conclusion of a video program in order to use it as the unit test. This way students are responsible for learning the requisite vocabulary from the early portions of the program. For once, the task that students are asked to accomplish in a test environment corresponds precisely to real-life situations.

Perhaps the greatest challenge at the lower levels lies in locating appropriate video materials. As long as you keep in mind two basic principles already mentioned, however, your task will be simplified: you need not find entire programs that are suitable from beginning to end for lower-level students, and you can manipulate the intelligibility of the program either by preparing the tape or by preparing the students. Use video well in your lower-level courses and you can be sure that you will produce students who will be eager to see how you use video materials in your upper-level courses.

Practical Suggestions

"Principles are fine," a colleague once quipped, "but they are not very good at running a ditto machine." However important principles may be, they cannot be counted on to devise the activities and exercises on which day-to-day language instruction is based. In order to provide grammar practice, to sensitize students to cultural differences, and to provoke active language production, language instructors must spend a great deal of time and effort devising pedagogically viable exercises and activities. This section suggests numerous strategies that instructors may use as models. In the interest of clarity, these exercises have been organized according to the five stages of video pedagogy: preliminary exercises, activities for out-of-class viewing, in-class strategies, review assignments, and video testing.

The examples in this section have been drawn from three programs especially suited for use in lower-level language courses. From France comes *Télématin*, a version of the popular Antenne 2 morning show specially reedited for use in first-year French courses. This hour-long program contains short segments of many types, including news, weather, short features, songs, public service announcements, how-to tips, and advertisements. Spanish is represented by *Ni en vivo ni en directo*, a series of comic skits featuring the popular comedian Emilio Aragón. Although it is only eleven minutes long, this program contains more than a dozen separate sketches. From the German-speaking world comes *Nachrichten I*, a compilation of reports from the evening TV news in East Germany, West Germany, and Austria. Each of the reports in *Nachrichten I* begins with an English-language introduction produced by the BBC and offers a choice of two sound tracks, the original sound track and a simplified voice-over text spoken more slowly than the original.

Preliminary Exercises

A hallmark of the integrated approach to video pedagogy is careful attention to the activities that precede the first viewing of a video program. Students who go abroad immediately encounter an expanded version of the foreign language they have learned in class, with richer vocabulary, faster speech, and more difficult accents. In recognition of this difficulty, American instructors regularly prepare their students for the foreign experience by stressing the knowledge and skills necessary for survival abroad. It is useful to think of the international video experience as a trip to a foreign country. What background do students need in order to derive the greatest benefit from the video? What aspects of the video are most likely to confuse students? Is there a way of alleviating that confusion? By considering questions like these as they construct the course syllabus, instructors ensure the creation of appropriate preliminary exercises. Since one goal of preliminary activities is to facilitate comprehension of the video program to come, these activities should be chosen according to the difficulties of a particular program and keyed to the purpose of the program within the course as a whole. Some examples of possible activities follow.

Reading Passages

The more authentic the video selection, the more likely that it will include terms not included in your textbook. The traditional approach to this problem lies in vocabulary lists or glossed transcripts. Students learn considerably more, however, from reading prior to viewing an appropriate passage that includes the potentially troublesome terms used in context. Even at the very lowest levels this principle holds true. A *Télématin* news and weather report accompanying a unit on use of prepositions with geographical terms might be preceded by a reading selection that includes nothing more than selected headlines and a European weather forecast. Even before students see the video they will be prepared to recognize, understand, and repeat the names of cities and countries mentioned by the announcers.

At a more advanced stage, the same approach continues to bear fruit. *Ni en vivo ni en directo* contains a hilarious parody of a news program, called **Reducción Abierta,** in which Emilio Aragón reports on a poll of parents asked if they know where their children are. The poll demonstrates, Aragón quips, that the children seem not to know where their parents are. Very little preparation is needed to help students understand the simple Spanish of this selection. Creative use of it to encourage oral language production, however, might involve requiring students to conduct their own poll and respond to each other's questions. Preliminary reading of a poll on evening activities in Spain will provide students the background they need to participate creatively in a classroom poll. Important vocabulary and grammar items will thus be reinforced by repeated exposure.

When appropriate images are available, the preliminary reading selection might well be replaced by some form of picture: a still from the video program to be viewed later, a map of the area covered by the video, a set of drawings giving students a series of clues about the video to come, or a comic strip treating a related topic. Even a rapid preview of the video itself may be used in this manner, with or without the sound track. Students who have some notion of what the words refer to will have a much easier time placing those words into an overall narrative context.

Written Exercises

Although preliminary reading selections are especially good for introducing difficult vocabulary and cultural information, they provide little opportunity for practice with important expressions and constructions. Well-devised written exercises, on the other hand, make it easy to concentrate attention on important aspects of the language. The fourth section of *Nachrichten I* reports on a gas price increase in Austria, thus providing welcome

One important function of the introduction to each news item in *Telejournal* is to facilitate student understanding of key terms, as in this list of petroleum product prices. (*Nachrichten I*)

aural practice with numbers and prices. Students who have difficulty with the German terms designating various petroleum products will be unable to concentrate on the price increases, however, and the figures provided by the announcer will not be understood by students who have failed to review the numbers between twenty and one hundred. An appropriate preliminary exercise would require students to calculate the price for so many liters of **Super, bleifrei** [lead-free], **Diesel,** or **Heizöl** [home heating oil]. In this way they will learn the gasoline terms necessary to understand the news report while they are practicing the very numbers needed to follow the account of price increases.

Many types of exercises can be used to produce similar results. When single words are targeted, they may be included in an exercise that requires students to identify the word that does not fit in a series of otherwise related terms, or they may be introduced in multiple-choice questions. When it is important that students become acquainted with a particular type of construction used in a video program, the construction in question may be regularly inserted into a series of true-false questions apparently unrelated to the video. In many cases, instructors will wish to encourage students to practice important vocabulary or syntactic patterns. They can easily accomplish this by use of a matching exercise or a series of questions to be answered in full written sentences, either independently or in response to a reading passage. For example, in preparation for a humorous treatment of Spanish road signs in *Ni en vivo ni en directo*, students might be given a page of road signs and asked either to match them to a list of meanings or to describe their meaning in sentence form. Students who have completed an exercise of this type will not only better understand the humor of the video sketch, they will also be better able to participate in a follow-up discussion of the program involving creation of their own humorous road signs.

Group Activities

In most cases, group activities grow out of video viewing. In some situations, however, group activities carried out before viewing can enhance the viewing experience. Both *Nachrichten I* and the news portions of *Télématin* mention many German and French geographical terms. The spelling and location of the cities, regions, and countries mentioned will be unfamiliar to many students. Although this problem could be handled by a reading selection or preliminary exercise, some instructors may wish instead to devise a map game designed to familiarize students not only with the spelling and location of the places in question but also with their *pronunciation*. A map showing only the geographical names that will be encountered in the upcoming video program will form the basis for many appropriate activities. For example, students might play a variation on the Grandmother's Trunk game. The first student mentions what he took with him to the first city ("When I went to Düsseldorf I took a towel with me"), the second student adds an item that she took to the nearest city among those on the map ("When I went to Bonn I took a towel and a toothbrush with me"), and so forth. Depending on the level of the class, the items carried might come from a list of objects found in the video program or might be freely chosen. Any number of alternatives to this activity may be devised.

Out-of-Class Viewing Activities

Preliminary exercises prepare students for maximum comprehension of a specific video program. Out-of-class viewing activities assure a carefully targeted use of the program itself by requiring students to alternate between viewing a video sequence and completing a related written activity. Where possible, students will engage in out-of-class viewing activities primarily in the language lab, either individually or in small groups. Where no language lab facilities exist, exercises may be modified to suit a scheduled out-of-class viewing for the entire class. Although this alternative all but precludes frequent starting and stopping of the tape, it does provide students with more opportunity to concentrate on their own workbook exercises than is possible in the typical classroom situation. Out-of-class viewing activities might usefully be organized into the following categories:

VCR and Program Familiarity Exercises

In institutions where students have individual access to a VCR, it is important to provide training in the use of the machines, as well as experience in locating the proper segments of a tape that includes multiple items. This training may conveniently be carried out in the early stages of the beginning course, when students are learning numbers. A typical exercise would be written in the target language, perhaps with some terms glossed, to familiarize students with all the terms necessary for describing the functioning of the VCR. In translation, such an exercise might look like this:

1. Turn on the VCR with the button on the left.
2. Set the counter on the right to 000.
3. Use the fast-forward control to advance to 083. How many men and women do you see on the screen?
   _____ men _____ women
4. Use the visual advance to go to 126. What time is it on the clock on the screen? _____
5. Use the fast reverse to go to 102. What time is it now?
   _____
6. Advance to the first advertisement. What is the number on the counter? _____
7. Look at your video guide. Find the news, first in the guide and then on the tape. What is the counter number?
   _____

An alternative approach, especially appropriate for programs like *Nachrichten I*, *Ni en vivo ni en directo*, and *Télématin*, which are constructed of many independent segments, is to provide students with a partial list of the segments on the tape. Students are then asked to discover the name of the news items or segment titles missing from the list. Carefully conceived exercises of this type can prepare students not only to use the VCR properly but eventually to talk about video more easily in the target language.

Recognition Exercises

Just as sounds and segmentation constitute the basis of linguistic comprehension, so the recognition of discrete words is an important initial aspect of understanding video. Early viewing exercises should provide concentrated work on this potential stumbling block. At first it is best to set rather simple aural tasks for students. When the students are learning numbers, for example, they may be asked to listen to a short program, note the numbers they hear, and identify who says them. When a new verb tense is introduced, students may be asked to list the verbs they hear in that tense, spell them properly, and indicate the person and number. For new vocabulary, students can be given a list of words and asked to identify the ones they hear in the program, to place them in the order in which they are spoken on the video, or to match them with the characters who say them. Exercises like this help students begin their video experience positively. Instead of thinking about how difficult the language is, they concentrate on a specific problem that they are perfectly capable of solving. As they learn to recognize specific terms or constructions, students will little by little develop the skills necessary for understanding the message as a whole.

At a more advanced level, recognition exercises may be coupled with other concerns. Students watching the *Télématin* ski report presented earlier in this chapter might be encouraged to identify which of two phrases they have heard. The alternatives offered might systematically propose an informal and a formal way of stating the same information, as follows:

1. **En ski, ben, les Suisses dominent tout.**
   [Um, in skiing, the Swiss are winning everything.]
   En ski, les Suisses restent dominants.
   [In skiing, the Swiss remain dominant.]

2. **Cette fois, c'est fini, elle a remis les pendules à l'heure.**
   [This time it's over, she's reset the clocks.]
   Lors de la dernière compétition, ce défaut a été corrigé.
   [In the latest competition this problem has been eliminated.]

3. **Ecoutez, écoutez la charmante Maria.**
   [Listen, listen to the charming Maria.]
   Voilà ce que dit Mademoiselle Walliser.
   [Here is what Miss Walliser said.]

This exercise provides important ear training for students but at the same time lays the groundwork for classroom discussion about language levels and the difference between formal and informal discourse.

Comprehension Exercises

From the beginning, students should be encouraged to strive for comprehension. In the early weeks of an initial course, however, care must be taken to ask students for the kind of comprehension that they can reasonably be expected to achieve. There are a number of possible ways of reaching this goal. Students might be asked, for example, to answer a series of true-false questions about a *Télématin* newscast. Not only do true-false questions usually require only minimal understanding, but they have the virtue of providing the vocabulary necessary for comprehension of the video. Students are thus helped along by the questions themselves as they learn the spelling of the terms on the tape. Another exercise might offer a list of statements that include strategically placed errors, which students are required to correct. Some of the errors will relate to the image and others to the dialogue, so that students will note the relationship between the two. As students develop greater skill in listening and writing, they might be encouraged to answer questions, read before viewing, about the video program. A careful choice of questions in an exercise of this kind will help to prepare students for a focused class discussion.

For instructors using video for the first time, the temptation is great to rely heavily on a word-for-word transcript of the video. The transcript apparently dissipates the fear shared by many that students will not understand the chosen video program. Out of this transcript-oriented approach typically grow Cloze exercises, in which students fill in the blanks in a partial transcript, and other exercises that depend more on the transcript than on the video tape. The problem with using a transcript is that it provides students with a crutch that discourages them from developing the skills necessary to understand the oral language. I suggest that transcripts be left for more advanced courses. At the lower levels it is best to concentrate on specifically targeted concerns, as with the number, verb tense, and vocabulary recognition exercises already suggested, or on broad understanding of general aspects. In order to foster and check the latter, you might provide students with an incomplete summary of the actions in a specific video segment and ask them to fill in the missing portions. *Ni en vivo ni en directo* includes a delightful song spoofing the Spanish chaperone tradition. In each segment, Emilio Aragón participates in an activity with his sweetheart, **y su madre también** [and her mother too]. An exercise scrambling the segments or leaving some out not only calls for achievable comprehension from the students, but simultaneously provides important vocabulary in support of that comprehension.

As students develop the ability to understand the oral language, they may be asked more complex questions that assume understanding rather than testing for it. Such questions often ask "Why?" rather than "What happened?" Questions on the opening section of *Nachrichten I* might concentrate on why the inhabitants of Düsseldorf are especially proud of their train station; students viewing a weather forecast might be asked which parts of the country would be appropriate for sunbathing or skiing. Carefully composed questions of this type do more than check comprehension. They also concentrate students' attention on aspects of the video that you plan to discuss in class or on the grammar, vocabulary, or cultural concerns that you wish to highlight. For example, plot summary exercises can encourage practice of almost any verb form, and content questions can stress any aspect of vocabulary. Even cultural concerns can be highlighted by out-of-class viewing exercises.

Cultural Awareness Exercises

Often combined with comprehension exercises, cultural awareness activities serve to make the most of video's authentic cultural representations. The most obvious approach is to ask students to identify objects or practices that differ from their familiar American counterparts. Although this strategy remains useful, it does have the potential drawback of defining everything in relation to American practice. With *Nachrichten I*, one might instead take advantage of the presentation of different German regions in the feature on **Dreikönigstag** [Epiphany] to ask students to note differences between Oberammergau and Bremen. The differing accents of the various announcers on *Télématin* might be used to sensitize students to differences in pronunciation. Students will become better observers of cultural particularities if they have been encouraged by individual exercises to develop the skills necessary to cultural observation. Exercises might thus be devised that ask students to pay special attention to speech patterns, body relationships, signs and posters, class relations, eating habits, and other important cultural aspects. One of the most satisfactory cultural exercises involves the use of authentic application documents from the target culture. Students who fill out a German passport application, a French Social Security medical reimbursement form, or a Spanish **libro de familia** [a booklet delivered by a priest to a married couple for registering births and deaths in the family] learn rapidly about another culture. Filling out one of these forms for a character in a video program provides in addition a rapid comprehension check. Such an activity would be especially appropriate for use with the segment of *Ni en vivo ni en directo* that depicts Emilio Aragón's frustrations at the **Registro Civil** [Registry of Civil Records].

Group Activities

One of the most exciting aspects of video is the opportunity it offers for successful small-group activities. While these are not possible in every situation or with every group, they have such enormous educational potential that they are worth fostering. Many fruitful small-group activities involve regularly stopping the tape at a point that will encourage oral production by the students. For example, one student might sit next to the monitor, or hold the remote control, and stop the tape whenever he or she recognizes a word from a prescribed category, such as an article of clothing, a reflexive verb, or the time of day. Let us suppose that the category chosen is numbers above one hundred. When the first student stops the tape, the second must identify the number just spoken, the third must give the next highest number in sequence, and the fourth the next lowest. Geographical terms might then be pointed out, with the first student stopping the tape, the second identifying the term just spoken, the third naming the country in which the place is located, and the fourth naming the continent. Parts of the body, too, could be identified with one student stopping the tape, another identifying the term just pronounced, still another naming a part of the body adjacent to the one first named, and so on. This kind of activity can easily be adapted for groups of any size, working on nearly any lesson, with virtually any tape. In the classroom, this type of activity could take the form of a competition between two teams.

In-class Viewing Strategies

In many cases, the exercises suggested for out-of-class viewing can also be used in class. As a rule, however, class time should be reserved for activities that can be carried out only in class or that derive particular benefit from the presence of the instructor. In-class activities are thus listed here according to the reason for choosing to carry them out in class, rather than in some other context.

Lively Interaction with the Video Program

When students watch a videotape they tend to watch it as they would a film or a television program, never stopping the tape until the very end. One of the important roles the intructor can play is that of an animator who energizes students and assures more lively interaction with the video program. The instructor thus carries the responsibility for activating aspects of video to which access is provided by no other situation. The exercises that fulfill this function are those in which the instructor serves as an active mediator between screen and students, stopping the tape often and asking questions about what the students have seen or heard. The teacher, as something of a master of ceremonies for the variety show provided by the video, must know how to make each new act appear especially exciting and desirable.

In many cases, this involves nothing more than what teachers have always done: bring energy and excitement to the classroom. Sometimes it takes specific recognition that students have had enough of one kind of work and that it is time for variety. With video, variety is easy to achieve. Even within a single sequence, it is not difficult to move from phonetics to vocabulary or from grammar to culture. In some cases, the simple act of stopping the tape facilitates specific exercises. When the tape is stopped, time is implicitly divided into three parts: the part of the program already seen, the time that the class spends talking about the program, and the part of the program still to come. This tripartite division makes it particularly easy to ask students questions that require a response in a specific tense. One of the early segments of *Ni en vivo ni en directo*, for example, takes place at an auto mechanic's garage. Stopping the tape as Emilio Aragón begins to vacuum out a car still occupied by the driver, the teacher can easily ask a question requiring an answer in a designated tense.

1. **Present.** What is the mechanic wearing?
2. **Past.** Where did the mechanic come from?
3. **Future.** What will he do next?
4. **Conditional.** If the vacuum came too close to the woman's dress, what would happen?
5. **Subjunctive.** What do you want to see happen?

With a little imagination and forethought, instructors can assure through video a lively class period without abandoning any of the traditional goals of language teaching.

Informed Teacher Commentary

One drawback of individual student viewing is that it tends to reinforce misunderstanding or poor listening habits. If the student cannot hear an essential word at the beginning of the program, there is no assurance that he or she will be able to hear it at the end. Classroom alternation between a video sequence and a commentary by teacher or students provides a corrective to the potential misunderstanding of individual students. For a unit on telling time, for example, a first-year French teacher might use randomly chosen sections of *Télématin*, asking students to tell the time from the clock that remains visible in the lower right-hand corner throughout the program.

Teacher commentary can also help students correct faulty grammar or pronunciation. Using first a familiar segment and later a sequence chosen at random, students can be asked to listen for and identify *any* question that they recognize. Students could then be asked to explain how they knew it was a question, to which they might respond: "I heard **est-ce que.**" "I heard **comment.**" "I could tell by the tone." When nobody in the class recognizes a question, it is important to play the passage again, so that the best students may benefit from the instructor's experience, just as the weaker students will certainly learn from the better ones.

Instructors may appropriately put their cultural expertise to work in the same way. One good way to do this is to ask students to note

Programs with a clock afford constant opportunity for work with time, temporal expressions, and varied tenses. This news presentation from *Télématin* reveals the familiar outlines of the city of Paris.

cultural particularities during an out-of-class viewing. During class time they may be asked to share their cultural observations. The instructor may corroborate the student's perception and place it in a larger context, perhaps explaining why or how the practice in question developed, or demonstrate that the apparent cultural particularity is in fact only a local practice, an anachronism, or an imprecision in the program. Unless students' cultural perceptions are checked in this way from time to time, even the heightened authenticity of the video medium will be unable to assure the desired cultural awareness.

Monitored Oral Production

Instructors' knowledge is especially important in the realm of oral language. Whereas out-of-class exercises can easily check comprehension, they rarely provide an opportunity to correct students' pronunciation or other oral habits. In a classroom situation, however, the instructor can easily monitor oral production. Many of the exercises suggested for use during out-of-class viewing may be used to elicit appropriate in-class oral production. Depending on the level of students involved, the exercises may stress the image, broad narrative concerns, or detailed understanding and re-production of sound track material. To focus on the image alone, for example, the instructor might use an exercise in which each student in turn must identify by name one object on the screen, while another must make a sentence using the word in question. To exploit broad narrative aspects, the instructor might have students reconstruct the story line or tell parts of the story in reverse order, using the future tense, or from the point of view of a particular character. To produce more careful attention to specific aspects of the spoken language, the instructor might use an exercise that requires students to recognize and present information communicated through the sound track but not available through the image alone.

The relatively formal aspect of the classroom setting can also be used to good effect in encouraging oral production. Students might be asked to prepare their own voice-overs for one of the sections of a videotape regularly used by the class. Each student would deliver a narration in class, with the TV volume turned all the way down. A presentation of this type gives students practice in producing language that, while oral, must remain relatively formal. In many cases, the video situation itself will suggest appropriate role-playing activities. *Nachrichten I* reports that gas prices went up in Austria at midnight. With this sequence you might have students play the roles of a gas station attendant explaining the new prices and an irate motorist who has had to wait in line from ten before to ten past midnight. With the **Registro Civil** routine from *Ni en vivo ni en directo*, in which Emilio Aragón has troubles first at a government window and then at a post office window, students might be asked to act out typical encounters at other familiar windows: railroad, theater, cinema, passport, customs, and bank. Another role-playing activity appropriate for the oral proficiency classroom might start with a viewing of the numerous examples of greeting in *Télématin*. Pass out role slips to pairs of students, designating a series of relationships, such as mother-daughter, male student–female student, and secretary-employer. Have the members of each pair greet each other in an appropriate way, with the class as a whole responsible for recognizing their relationship, perhaps from a list provided.

Animated Group Activities

Many of the most exciting foreign video activities simply will not work without a group of people. The song sung by Emilio Aragón in *Ni en vivo ni en directo* provides a clear case in point. Riding in a car, on a picnic, kissing, jogging, even in their honeymoon bed, the loving couple

A humorous video can be used to motivate students to increased class participation, as well as to understand what is humorous to another culture. This scene shows the Spanish comic actor Emilio Aragón, who repeatedly finds himself with his fiancée **y su madre también** (and her mother too). (*Ni en vivo ni en directo*)

is never without the girl's mother. Each time the refrain arrives, "and her mother too," students howl with delight, even if they have only partially understood the preceding verse. When students exhibit this kind of excitement, instructors do well to take advantage of it. They can easily do so by asking individual students to create sentences to which the other students will echo the familiar refrain, **y su madre también.** Eventually the refrain might be changed as well, to provide practice with possessive adjectives. This is an ideal activity to use early in the year, because it gives even the weakest students the opportunity to produce authentic and meaningful language.

Many activities that can be carried out by individuals are more successfully done in a group. In an individual exercise, each student might be given a slip of paper showing the name of some object or action that will appear in an upcoming video sequence. Once the student has discovered the item in question, he or she is asked to create a sentence using the word on the slip of paper. This exercise is far more satisfying, however, if students identify their objects or actions as the tape rolls along and then form groups of two or three in order to write sentences. This time, the sentences must contain the words of all those in the group. After they have read the first sentences, the students are combined in different groups and produce yet another round of sentences, this time with a new mix of words.

The presence of other students provides a very real incentive for accurate communication. Foreign video provides students with a constant diet of international geography. You can successfully turn this into appropriate oral production by asking students to explain to other students an itinerary that you have drawn on a map, using cities or regions mentioned in the video program. With a city map, students might be instructed to give street directions. With a map of the country that marks the location of cities but does not name them, students might be told to use city names. With a road map, students might use directions and distances or highway numbers. In each case, the important point is that one student must communicate with another using the language alone.

Review Assignments

Review exercises are designed to accomplish a number of specific goals: (a) to make sure that certain basic cultural facts will be remembered, (b) to help students retain useful vocabulary important to the video but not specifically taken up in the textbook, (c) to give students added practice using the knowledge and skills fostered by the video materials. None of these notions are new. Whether video work or more traditional text work is being reviewed, the principles are fundamentally the same. Review activities are conveniently treated according to the type of skill highlighted.

Recognition

Having learned how to recognize a specific grammatical structure or vocabulary item in a familiar video program, students should be challenged to recognize the same features in an unfamiliar program. The program used for review purposes might be one that students will study in detail later in the course, or it might be one that presents new linguistic variations or cultural particularities. However the new program is chosen, viewing it will reinforce an important principle: one of the best ways to review video work is through video.

Video programs with two different sound tracks provide a special opportunity for creative review. Because it includes a simplified sound track complementing the voice of the original announcer, *Nachrichten I* invites an incremental teaching pattern, beginning with the simplified sound track and progressing to the relatively more difficult German of the original newscast. Because the two sound tracks use much of the same vocabulary and some of the same grammatical constructions, the more rapid delivery of the original announcer provides a perfect check on the recognition and comprehension abilities of students who can understand the simplified version with little difficulty.

Manipulation

Review exercises aimed at manipulation of targeted grammar forms or cultural knowledge are a familiar component of all courses. To the traditional workbook exercises, video-oriented instructors might add classroom activities designed to encourage students to manipulate previously studied material. Instead of asking students to transform a sentence from the video into a different tense in writing, the instructor might stop a familiar video at the end of each sentence and have students orally perform the required transformation. Many exercises benefit from the broad, improvised nature of this kind of review, as long as students are fully familiar with the video segments chosen.

Review activities aimed at manipulation can make effective use of props derived from the video program itself. A map and a set of magnetic, velcro, or felt numbers and weather symbols creates a stage on which students can manipulate many aspects of their video-inspired knowledge: weather vocabulary, days of the week, geographical terms and appropriate accompanying prepositions, future and past tenses, numbers. By successively combining role-playing activities based on one video program with the vocabulary and cultural knowledge derived from a previous program, instructors can assure a continuing review of important areas.

Production

Between manipulation and production there is but a nuance. Whereas manipulation exercises foster relatively predictable use of familiar material within a limited framework, production activities aim at weaning students from the familiar context, encouraging them to use targeted knowledge in a broader range of situations. Students who have written advertising copy in imitation of TV ads they have just viewed might at a later date be asked to devise advertisements based on the vocabulary and structures acquired since the earlier assignment. While providing useful review, this type of activity also encourages students to integrate diverse sorts of knowledge into their own production.

Practically speaking, almost any activity appropriate for eliciting language production based on the current video program can be used at a later date for review. A particularly productive approach involves repeated use of the same basic framework as a review device and production incentive. Users of *Ni en vivo ni en directo*, for example, might regularly use the basic situation of the **Registro Civil** segment, in which one person comes up to a post office or other window and asks questions of the functionary in charge. With each new set of vocabulary or each new grammar area, and after each new video program, students might be encouraged to play the same basic roles, but with a modified topic and situation. After a geography lesson or video on Venezuela, the dialogue might involve a traveler and a travel agent. For past tenses, a police report on a missing person might serve as model. After a video segment stressing clothes—like the sequence at the beginning of *Ni en vivo ni en directo*, in which a mechanic vacuums up a woman's dress— a dialogue might take place at the catalogue order desk of a major Madrid clothing store. French classes using *Télématin* could build a similar continuity of production-oriented review around the newscast, with each new video or reading passage being reported by classroom newscasters. Students working with *Nachrichten I*, familiar with the availability of two sound tracks for each sequence, original and simplified, will benefit from producing their own simplified sound tracks for subsequent videos. As long as they are used in combination with other approaches, repeated exercises like these give students a sense of continuity and a head start on language production, while reducing the time necessary to describe new activities.

Video Testing

Two primary functions are fulfilled by video testing. From the very beginning of video use, testing informs the instructor about the students' level of understanding, thus providing important input into future decisions about appropriate activities. Furthermore, throughout the course, video testing constitutes a method of evaluation central to the grading process. Although both functions often play a role in the same test, their goals are sufficiently different to merit separate treatment.

Diagnostic Testing

It would be hard to overemphasize the importance of instructors' remaining aware of their students' level of understanding. Video work done outside of class involves too many variables to serve adequately for evaluative purposes. Nor does most class discussion suffice, since it is often dominated by the best students or those who are most gifted aurally. Instructors can easily remain aware of current comprehension levels by giving regular, short, ungraded quizzes early in the period during which a particular program is used. These quizzes should test students' understanding of previously viewed video material as well as their ability to recognize or understand targeted terms in unfamiliar video programs. By varying the number of times a video segment is played, instructors can also gain some insight into the difference between performance levels after first hearing and after multiple hearings.

Diagnostic testing need not be long or complicated. You might, for example, ask students to note each number they hear, along with the noun modified by that number, in a two-minute sequence of a familiar program. Then you might ask them to perform the same task using two minutes of an unfamiliar program of similar difficulty, with the first minute played twice and the second minute played only once. This kind of test is short, provides maximum information, and serves simultaneously as a teaching device. Furthermore, it stands little chance of scaring students. On the contrary, it accustoms them to taking tests based on the video itself, an important secondary function of diagnostic testing.

A later diagnostic test might emphasize cultural concerns rather than vocabulary or grammar. Students might be asked to identify in a short sequence from a familiar program three objects or practices particular to the culture in question. Then they might be asked to do the same thing with an unknown program. Besides revealing problem areas to the instructor, this type of test reminds students of the importance of cultural study within overall course priorities.

Proficiency Assessment

For institutional as well as intellectual reasons, comparative evaluation of individual students must be provided in most courses. Ungraded quizzes are useful teaching and diagnostic devices, but students need to understand that, no matter how much fun the video is, it is also serious work for which they will be held responsible. Fundamental guidelines for video assessment differ little from those practiced in more traditional situations. The areas evaluated should have been stressed in the course and should be essential for subsequent use of the language. The type of test chosen must be clear and should correspond to the kind of work already required.

If you have already used dictation exercises based on material from a video program, then dictation can provide an appropriate approach to testing sounds and segmentation. Aural recognition exercises based on the video itself are also useful in this regard. You can easily test active knowledge of vocabulary by asking students to write a description of a short video sequence or a treatment appropriate for a newscast or other discursive situation. Strategies for grammar testing depend on the targeted areas, but a useful approach involves asking students to answer specific questions as they view a video sequence, with the questions written in such a way as to assure that the answers will use the targeted forms. After a weather forecast used to complement a unit on geographical terms, for example, students might be asked a series of questions for which the video furnishes the following answers: **à** Lyon, **en** France, **la** Suisse, **au** Danemark, **en** Normandie, **aux** Etats-Unis, and so forth. To test how well students recognize the importance of differing discursive situations, the instructor might have students rewrite a short dialogue, perhaps substituting a pair of school friends for the two strangers in the video. Students will be expected to make appropriate changes in level of discourse. Cultural understanding can be tested in many different ways. Even without recourse to video viewing, students can be asked to explain or exemplify specific cultural practices previously encountered in a video program. The presence of the video itself opens up many other testing possibilities, from simple "What is it?" questions to more sophisticated queries about the origin or importance of a particular practice.

This chapter has suggested various ways of exploiting video in lower-level language courses. It goes without saying that the suggestions made here fall far short of exhausting the possibilities. Throughout the chapters to come are other suggestions that may be used in the early stages of language learning, as long as appropriate modifications are made for beginning students.

Notes

1. E. Jensen and T. Vithner suggest that three to seven minutes is the right length in their article "Authentic versus Easy Conflict in Foreign Language Material—a Report on Experiences with Production and Exploitation of Video in FLT," *System*, 7, No. 2 (1983), 261–75. Although I agree with the general tenor of their recommendations, I would point out that the appropriate length is highly dependent on the type of material and the level of the class. Later chapters will provide more information about these parameters.

2. Teachers often assume that advertisements are free from legal concerns—indeed, that instructors are providing a service by showing the ads. In some sense, teachers may be enhancing the reputation of the product, but they should remember that ads, like other texts, are written, directed, and acted by individuals who have the right to profit from

their work. These people have agents who insist most vehemently that their clients' rights be respected to the letter.

3. It might also be useful to see how others have adapted TV ads to educational purposes. See, for example, Gerald Honigsblum, *97 Publicités télévisées: Le français en réclame* (Lexington, Mass.: Heath, 1987), and Katherine D. Lawrence, "The French TV Commercial as a Pedagogical Tool in the Classroom," *French Review,* 60, No. 6 (May 1987), 835–44.

4. See in particular Jean-Pierre Berwald, "Teaching French Language Skills with Commercial Television," *French Review,* 50, No. 2 (December 1976), 222–26; "Teaching Foreign Language Skills by Means of Subtitled Visuals," *Foreign Language Annals,* 12, No. 5 (1979), 375–80; "Teaching French via Driver Education," *Foreign Language Annals,* 13, No. 5 (1980), 205–208; "Video and Second Language Learning," *Studies in Language Learning,* 5, No. 1 (1985), 3–16; and *Au Courant: Teaching French Vocabulary and Culture Using the Mass Media* (Washington, D.C.: Center for Applied Linguistics, 1986), especially Chapter 12, "Commercial Television." See also Louis A. Olivier, "Using 'Off-Air' Television Broadcasts from Non-U.S. Sources—Some Practical Suggestions," *Studies in Language Learning,* 5, No. 1 (1985), 45–52.

5. Thanks to a program of support from the Annenberg/Corporation for Public Broadcasting Project, the Project for International Communication Studies is currently developing a series of support materials to help teachers exploit international video programs.

6. Alice C. Omaggio, *Teaching Language in Context: Proficiency-Oriented Instruction* (Boston: Heinle & Heinle, 1986), 105ff.

7. Jean-Pierre Berwald, "Video and Second Language Learning," *Studies in Language Learning,* 5, No. 1 (1985), 7.

CHAPTER 5
Composition and Conversation Courses

What are composition and conversation courses? Aren't all language courses aimed at least in part at helping students to improve their speaking and writing skills? Because these terms are not entirely appropriate, the title of this chapter is to some degree misleading. More accurately stated, the subject here is the use of video programs to foster productive skills in the upper reaches of a language program, including fourth- and fifth-year and advanced placement courses in high school and college courses beyond the second year. It goes without saying that many of the approaches suggested in Chapter 4 are applicable to composition or conversation courses, just as many of the activities presented in this chapter may be adapted for use at an earlier level. With a little imagination, you can find a way to use video throughout your program to encourage more lively language production.

Successful approaches to student language production depend heavily on students' attitudes toward both their own abilities and the kind of language they are asked to produce. A badly selected video program can compound these problems by subjecting students to excessively difficult language or by encouraging discussion and writing of a particularly abstruse nature. In contrast, a well-selected video program offers special opportunities for encouraging student language production. Not only does video provide a far broader sampling of language types than the print media typically used in production-oriented courses, but it also supplies programs that are especially attractive to a generation raised on American TV.

Video's cultural component also serves as a special attraction. To be sure, overused expressions like "perspective on politics" or "the news in depth" are little more than clichés. However, television materials from other countries *literally* open up new perspectives and show us the local scene in depth. Whether novelistic or journalistic, written accounts tend to focus students' attention on a specific narrative. With video programs, the narrative retains its interest but is complemented by a broader audio-visual context. Often the background will catch the eye of a student otherwise hardly intrigued by a video program. Where a Spaniard might see only a newsworthy incident, an American student will be captivated by the passing cars, the fruit stands, and the billboards. No other medium offers so many opportunities to create a positive student attitude toward language production.

Composition

By and large, composition courses, or the composition component of more general courses, operate in the following manner. Students are exposed to a set of semantic and syntactic possibilities, usually expressed by a list of vocabulary terms or special grammar lessons and a reading selection. The students then produce a written document to practice their new semantic and syntactic acquisitions. In traditional courses, then, students read a passage, and write what amounts to a pastiche, whether it is so described to them or not. The students are expected to slide both vocabulary and grammar from the receptive side to the productive side. One of the very real problems with such an approach in the past has been the stilted nature of the resultant writing. Third-year students end up trying to write like André Gide, Thomas Mann, or Miguel de Unamuno, with little notion of the way French, German, or Spanish people commonly write or speak.

Video permits a new sensitivity to the oral language, to salutations and slang, to everyday, contemporary topics as well as to the eternal truths of classic literary texts. Video thus provides an invitation to experiment with new types of writing: newscasts, documentary voice-over presentations, interviews, advertisement copy, serial scripts, and the like. A video approach to writing is not meant to supplant familiar reading-oriented approaches but to complement them in particular ways according to video's special nature. Unless you are working with unusual students, you are likely to find that video serves as a strong motivating factor. Most of today's students do not dream of writing a prize-winning novel, nor do they pour their innermost thoughts into a diary; fame and fortune in the world of image and sound is what many long for. Instead of fighting this impulse, why not turn it to our advantage?

Video supplies a series of versatile generic models that can profitably be used as the basis for student writing. Have you noticed that most composition topics encourage students to write entirely in either the third or the first person? The following video models can induce broader use of the second person:

1. The interview format obliges students to use the first and second persons, with the designated interlocutors and the topic itself determining whether first-person plural and third-person forms will also be present.

2. A courtroom scene, with questioning and cross-examination, certainly covers every verb form.

3. The elaboration of a police report, from questioning of witnesses and suspects to the drafting of final copy, gives students the opportunity to use varied persons and tenses.

Perhaps you would like to shake your students out of the present tense. Although you may have been doing this for years by selecting topics that require the past tense, the following video programs make it easier to focus on any desired tense or mode:

1. Advertisement copy for video images is fun to write. It motivates students to deal with products from the target culture and makes the imperative—well, imperative.

2. Game shows, with their uncertainty and speculation, are perfect for concentrating attention on if clauses with the future tense ("If I win the money, I will . . . ") or even the past tense ("If I had won the car, I would have . . . ").

3. Contest shows seem made for interrogatives.

4. Weather forecasts require the future.

5. News reporting makes distinction among various past tenses necessary for comprehension.

In a way, all these examples are simply the video extension of the type of imagination teachers of composition have been exercising for years. Video expands the opportunities, but the principles remain the same.

There is an area, though, in which video opens radically new perspectives for composition subjects. Traditionally, teaching has depended on the artifacts of high culture: literature, literary language, and the type of civilization that appears to merit comparison with Greece or Rome. With the rise of the *Annales* school of "New History," however, we have become less interested in the spectacular events and individuals who remain from nation to nation surprisingly similar. We are increasingly concerned by the daily events that distinguish one people from another. From Charlemagne to Grace Kelly, high culture is marked by individuals characterized by their ability to thrive in any culture and classes marked by their tendency to borrow the best from other civilizations. I am less and less interested in the Monte Carlos of the world and more and more intrigued by the daily life of people. I want to know not just about the capital, but about the provinces, not just the official language but the creoles, the patois, and the acronyms. I want to know not just about the legislature but about the farms, the factories, and the fisheries.

To get at this unofficial realm through traditional literary texts is almost impossible. Part of the mystery and the wonder of popular culture lies precisely in its ability to avoid the formal world of statistics, texts, and literature. To be sure, the provinces exist in many national literatures, but all too often as viewed from the capital. The youth is often portrayed as viewed by the adult; the poor, as viewed by the landowner. The printed word is simply not the medium of slang, of song, and of protest. The video medium, on the other hand, is marvelously capable of capturing these seemingly nonstandard expressions of a popular culture (which actually constitute a more common type of civilization than the so-called standard culture itself). To be sure, television often distorts the common culture, yet it has the power to represent this culture more clearly than any other medium. How do people speak? What do they do with their bodies while they speak? When does slang replace the standard language? Well-chosen international television materials are capable of sensitizing

Video reveals cultural topics often ignored by standard textbooks, as in this video still of Senegalese farmers flailing grain in Francophone Africa. (*Fleuve Sénégal*)

For a Spaniard, this sequence from *Ni en vivo ni en directo* high-lights Emilio Aragón's irreverent humor; for an American student, it reveals a great deal about cultural and linguistic practices, from road signs and gastronomic preferences to present participles and gender roles. (*Ni en vivo ni en directo*)

students to these areas. Instead of accepting the stereotype from a poster as fact, students will become aware by watching carefully selected video materials of the variety of accents, interests, and types of expression that characterize a particular culture.

How, in practice, do we take advantage of television's democratizing tendencies? Perhaps the most obvious way is to profit from the increasing variety of subjects available on tape. The breadth of available coverage is striking and will certainly continue to grow. This variety will undoubtedly prove most useful in sensitizing students to the important cultural differences between countries. For example, the West German video series *Ein kurzes Leben lang* presents scenes from the life of a typical North German family. Each episode reveals new details about daily life in the region. The episode entitled "Putz dir die Schuhe ab" gives students a firsthand view of the importance of vocational education in Germany. Students who have seen this program might be asked to write an essay about education from the point of view of a character in the narrative. Instead of using terminology appropriate to American schools, students will be encouraged to work with the terms and structures of the German educational system.

Even with lower-level students this strategy can be remarkably rewarding. One of the skits included in the Spanish program *Ni en vivo ni en directo* builds a comic routine around humorous variations on road signs. Consistently employing present participles, the signs pass from traditional texts like **Hombres Trabajando** [men working] to whimsical messages like **Mujer Haciendo Paella** [woman preparing paella], each one objectified by the image that follows. Students who view this sequence will gain a realistic picture of the format followed by Spanish road markings. A writing exercise requiring the students to create their own comic road signs will provide practice in use of the present participle in particularly authentic Spanish constructions.

Video is also strikingly capable of revealing the variations in language level that characterize modern speech. Imagine the difference between the dialogue written by a student who has read an article about French schools and the dialogue written by a student who has watched *Isabelle et Véronique ou les deux lycéennes*, a program that presents a straightforward, unromanticized view of the daily activities of two French high-school students. A traditional approach would offer students a transcript, a vocabulary list, and a set of questions on the content of the video. Instead, the following variation is suggested:

> Briefly describe the program to students. Then ask them to view the program once out of class, with class discussion to follow. They should be expected to answer the following questions as they view:
>
> 1. What topics are most important to these young women?
> 2. What are the key words in their dialogue?
> 3. What words do they use that might not be used by a teacher? a housewife? a mechanic? their professors?
> 4. What sentences are you not sure you understand?

Classroom activities can be built around specific trouble spots and the vocabulary used by the French students. For example, start the class by clarifying the sentences that students were unable to understand. Then have students use key words in oral sentences, either in response to questions about the tape, as part of a narrative reconstitution exercise, or through free association. Expose the students to the written version of the terms in question only after they have spoken at length. In this manner, you are encouraging proper ear training and placing preliminary emphasis on the oral nature of the French students' vocabulary. By the time your students are ready to write, they will have become far more sensitive to the specificity of the French students' oral expression than if they had started with a printed list of vocabulary and a transcript.

Here is another useful suggestion for turning video programs into especially attractive writing exercises. Imagine that you are a video producer and your students are part of a "program doctor" consulting firm. You have hired them to spruce up the parts of a show that you find lackluster. Provide each student with a program or excerpt and identify the section that you find unacceptable. If you specify the reasons for your reaction, you can easily aim students' efforts in a direction that corresponds to the course goals. For example, you might list criticisms such as "the language is too popular," "the interviewer does not ask enough personal questions," "the reporter provides too little statistical information." This approach can target specific concerns even more accurately if you provide a partial transcript as a model, with indications of the type of rewrite needed for the *missing* lines. The student must understand enough of the missing line to know what is to be replaced but receives specific guidance about the type of replacement necessary. In my experience, this kind of exercise works even better when students work in small groups on the writing. Here, as in most other successful approaches, the video serves as a catalyst to other, related activities, rather than remaining a passive purveyor of words and images.

Conversation

Conversation is of course not an alternative to composition but its constant companion. However true this may be in traditional circumstances, it is even more true with video, where the oral/aural nature of the medium serves as a constant invitation to conversation. The activities that make video a natural participant in the conversation course thus apply to video pedagogy in general, whether for beginners or advanced students. Nearly all the comments in this section should therefore be considered eminently transferable to the oral production aspects of other courses. The section begins with a discussion of the video conversation classroom and then proceeds to suggestions regarding the importance of small-group activities in conversation, with a final rubric dealing with hands-on video production.

The Conversation Classroom

Typically, conversation courses have been built around alternation between what might be called *intake* and *output*. The intake usually includes reading a carefully chosen passage as homework, and the output involves related in-class conversation production. Many familiar strategies have been used to motivate students to speak in class, including graded participation, an imminent test, a controversial reading passage, debate-oriented activities, and numerous other approaches. Whatever the chosen strategy, however, one aspect remains staunchly stable: the reading material is consumed the night before, and the oral production is supposed to take place during class.

With video this separation need no longer exist. Video-supported conversation classes work best when teacher, video, and students share the same space, but speak alternately. The manipulability of video permits a more flexible, more dynamic approach. A video program in the classroom, stopped at appropriate points and aided by proper preparation and questioning, can generate far more discussion than a text read the night before. The possibilities of such a shared-space approach are manifold.

1. Everything that can be done with a theatrical text can be done with a video program, and the video provides the useful addition of visual and auditory examples for student language production. Phonetic practice is enhanced by the presence, immediately before each student's speech, of an audiovisual model. Similarly, body language receives a new impetus from students' imitation of appropriate video characters.

2. When little snippets of the program are played, it becomes a simple matter to engender repetition, review, prediction, or discussion based on material that is still alive in the student's mind. "Who is that character?" "What did he do in the previous scene?" "Why didn't she use the familiar form with him in this scene?" "What difference is there between these two women?" "What do you expect to find around that corner?" "Would you have made the same decision under these circumstances?" "What's going on in the background here?" "What does the background action have to do with the overall theme of the story?" Possible questions are innumerable.

3. The video program can become the basis of a student competition. Each group is asked to watch for a different aspect of the current topic—for example, for slang versus formal language, for traditional versus modern aspects of current Europe, for leftist versus rightist behavior. With careful preparation and insistence on explanation of the noted characteristic, this technique will take students' attention away from the video itself and project it onto an effective educational game. Do not hesitate to switch from program to program so that students will recognize the difference in language characteristics from region to region, from country to country, and from genre to genre.

With little trouble, numerous other methods of using video to its fullest extent can be devised for the conversation classroom. More than any other single approach, group activities help video to stimulate oral language production.

Group Activities

For years we have been aware that the most effective conversation practice takes place not in a classroom but in an informal atmosphere, with students using the target language to *communicate* rather than simply to impress the teacher. Much of the extracurricular activity associated with foreign languages specifically aims at fostering such informal practice: German clubs, Spanish houses, French tables, foreign exchange programs, and so forth.

What with the apparent desirability of informal group conversation, it might seem odd that informal group work is not used more often in an educational situation. Two inherent contradictions have made it more than a little difficult to implement such group work. Informality is not easy to legislate; indeed, it is hard to imagine any *classroom* activity that could be fully informal. Worse still, most conversational activity requires the presence of an animator, someone who speaks the language well enough to keep the ball rolling and to provide adequate language models. In the past this has almost always implied that an instructor had to be present. However, the presence of an instructor is counterproductive to informality, unless the instructor is especially good at disguising himself or herself as a student. As a result, the goal of informal conversation has usually been achieved only through good fortune and for short periods of time, since everything that might be done to assure its continued existence tends to undermine it.

Under the proper conditions, however, video can solve many of the problems that made it so hard to create informal or semiformal conversational situations in the past. When I first started working with international video materials at the University of Iowa, our facilities were far from what they are now. Even though I assigned only short programs to a single class, I found that the Language Media Center had significant scheduling problems. One student would arrive only to find that another had just started watching the assigned program on the sole VCR/monitor setup. After a period of arranging scheduled showings, my colleagues and I were finally successful in permanently allocating a separate room for video viewing. The room contained a half-dozen VCR/monitor setups isolated from one another by sound-absorbing room dividers. I assumed that when a student found one monitor in use, he or she would check out a second copy of the same program and use another monitor.

However, to my surprise, as the days went by I began to notice a pattern. Student A would come in and start to work. When student B arrived, he or she and student A would exchange comments and then often decide to work together on the same VCR and monitor. The better the students knew each other, the more likely the decision to view in a group rather than individually. Students were informally scheduling their viewing so that they could work together. At first, I was a little disconcerted. In my own mind, video was primarily a self-pacing medium, one that would permit infinite replays according to individual need. What I saw and heard allayed my fears considerably. At first the students in small viewing groups tended to exchange comments in English, but as the months went by they began to use the target language in group communication. Depending on the level and motivation of the students and the point in the semester, some made a conscious effort to use only the target language, whereas others seemed to use target-language words only because they were especially available and appropriate.

It did not take long to decide to take advantage of this impetus toward informal conversation around the video program. If students like to watch in groups, and if they are moved to talk about the program they are watching, why not reorganize video-oriented activities and class organization to revolve around group viewing? The following suggestions are some results of the new approach. They are particularly appropriate for use with students who are sufficiently fluent to sustain conversation, but they certainly have potential applications at any level.

1. Try holding conversation classes in a room that accommodates multiple VCR/monitor setups. Divide the class up and have them work in small groups with different programs. The instructor's role in this situation can vary from simple participant in one group to interviewer or interviewee in each group alternately.

2. Assign students to carry out their viewing homework in small groups. If your language lab has a native speaker present at certain times of the day, try to schedule your students at that time, as much to get a report on the nature of students' conversation as to give students the benefit of the native speaker's contributions.

3. Devise exercises that take advantage of group viewing. These exercises should be aimed not so much at furthering students' comprehension and knowledge as at inducing students to participate actively in conversation around the video program. To be sure, some of the most important discussions will derive from the program itself, but you can help the conversation along by asking the right questions and suggesting appropriate activities. Remember that your goal is not to force students to speak but to create an atmosphere in which informal speech is most likely to occur.

What kinds of exercises or activities are most likely to foster conversation? In one sense, the same old ones: the good topics, the controversial concerns, the existential decisions. An atmosphere of communication can be created, however, by topics that are far less earth-shattering. The first requirement is simply that all students should be involved, early on and without any fear. Simple questions at the start are thus to be preferred to a direct entry into the existential. For this reason, some kind of game structure is useful at the beginning, even when it is built on material simpler in nature than the material you want to see stressed in the long run. Human relations being what they are, it is best not to depend on any activity that *requires* all students in turn to provide some target-language term. To students, the stress of knowing that they have to produce undermines the pleasure of knowing that their production will not be immediately evaluated by the teacher. (Students often fear each other's opinions more than that of the instructor.) Here are some techniques that might serve as models:

1. **Speak-While-the-Tape-is-Rolling Activities.** In order not to undercut the dynamic nature of video, you can use some activities that do not interrupt the program. These can be as simple as recognition of particular categories of words ("Repeat any slang term you hear") or somewhat more complex ("Point out examples of traditional culture within the modern city"). Since this technique stresses speed rather than complexity, it is usually best used as a warm-up exercise for getting students used to exercising their tongues and lips.

2. **Start-Again-Stop-Again Exercises.** Most activities fall into this category, in which the video provides a cue for the viewer to stop the tape in order to permit relevant commentary. One variation of this technique involves splitting students into teams, with one team responsible for stopping the video and asking a question and the other responsible for providing a response. Questions can be implicit and automatic (Team A stops the tape whenever a geographical term is used; team B must explain or locate the term) or made up on the spot (The individual who stops the tape asks a question about the apparel worn by one of the characters).

3. **Video-and-Workbook Activities.** Just as the value of individual viewing can be considerably enhanced by well-prepared exercises, so group viewings can be guided and supported by workbook materials. These might be used in support of a game or competition—for example, a series of factual questions to be answered by two groups alternately—or as part of a more topically oriented approach—for example, a judgmental commentary on the tape, calling for counterjudgments. This approach works best if the instructor's questions turn students

into detectives eager to pay close attention to the program and to report their findings.

The group activities represented here are all designed to be carried out during actual viewing. Many other group activities are based on video work but not necessarily carried out during viewing. The next section describes one such activity.

Hands-on Production

Even if you are not a camera buff, some of your students probably are, and these days it is increasingly possible to obtain a simple, lightweight video camera. Video production is certainly not for everyone, and probably not for every course, but it can serve an especially important function in a conversation course. Video programs and video production can form a satisfying whole, each reinforcing the other. Furthermore, the production examples offered by short, simple television formats should be far more accessible than the more difficult cinematic model of narrative fiction.

One of the best things about video production is that it always serves as the crowning experience of a long and fruitful pedagogical progression. As such, the production activities go a long way toward automatically motivating students to do the research, writing, and conferring necessary for development of the final program. Let me suggest two totally different approaches to video production, each rewarding in its own way. The "news team" approach has the value of immediately valorizing familiar video material. Students begin with exercises that familiarize them with the various parts of the newscast. They then prepare their own interviews, weather reports, ads, and so forth outside of class and practice them in class. Finally, these activities are taped, viewed, and critiqued by the same students, now disguised as "network officials" or some other judgmental body. It is strikingly easy to get students interested in this work. To many instructors, the time and effort spent on the actual taping will seem fully worthwhile.

Another promising approach to hands-on video production involves a modern update of the familiar pen-pal exchange: instead of exchanging letters, two schools or classes exchange videotapes. The preparation of the videotape is of course more important than the tape itself. Students must discuss how they will conceive the videotape, what belongs in it, how they will assure continuity and coverage, and so forth. A script (dialogue or voice-over) or scenario must be prepared and a strategy for the actual filming developed. What is best about this approach is its discursive nature. Students are not just faking communication, they are planning a video letter to real people abroad. For some countries, the local consulate may help you find an appropriate partner. For French-speaking countries, the Bureau pour l'Enseignement de la Langue et de la Civilisation Françaises à l'Etranger (BELC) has established a video correspondence network. The network has its own newsletter, which includes practical suggestions and guidelines.[1] If your community is involved in an international exchange program, or if your school participates in any kind of study program abroad, you may want to consider setting up a video correspondence arrangement with your international partners, people whom your students actually know or will soon meet. Imagine the appeal of a yearly conversation course in which the shooting of a video letter is the ostensible ultimate goal—though the real goal is, of course, full involvement with the target language and culture. Even in lower-level courses, students can often learn a great deal from watching themselves on a TV screen. Why not have one class "shoot" another as part of a class project? There are significant logistical problems involved here, but the rewards are in many cases sufficient to justify the effort.

Notes

1. If you are interested in participating in a video correspondence with a French-speaking country, for further information please contact Micheline Maurice, Réseau Vidéo Correspondance, BELC, 9 rue Lhomond, 75005 Paris, France.

CHAPTER 6
Special-Purpose Language Courses

American language education has been heavily influenced by the goals of democracy. Many countries offer no language education at all to the vast majority of the population but provide a select few with an extremely high level of instruction in a second language. American educational theory, however, has always preferred to introduce most students to a foreign language but to carry almost none of them to a truly high level of excellence in that language. In spite of recent pleas for added concentration on the upper reaches of the language curriculum,[1] American language education resolutely retains its focus on basic language learning. This kind of language education teaches the principles of grammar rather than actual usage in a foreign country, stresses vocabulary with Latin roots rather than recent advertising phraseology, and limits itself to pointing out differences between cultures rather than going beyond this goal to teach students how to communicate effectively in another culture.

To be sure, an understanding of differences is an essential democratic virtue, but language teaching should go beyond this stage. We live in an increasingly international world. The number of Americans working and traveling abroad increases yearly, as does the percentage of foreign-born U.S. citizens. International markets, once spurned by American industry, are providing a growing number of internationally oriented jobs. Our curriculum *needs* to find more room for advanced language teaching, with courses that target specific aspects of a language.

Over the past decade, American schools have begun to offer such courses. Because of the importance of Spanish within the United States, many of these new courses are aimed at professionals working within the Spanish-speaking community: Spanish for agricultural purposes, Spanish for health professionals, and so forth. Development of business language courses has brought a new impetus to the upper reaches of the language curriculum for the other domains. Translation, once all but banned from language instruction, has also returned to the advanced language curriculum, spawning courses in commercial and technical translation or subtitling. These are the courses with which the current chapter is concerned. There are special-purpose language courses offered at a lower level—French for travelers, Spanish for survival, and Italian for opera lovers—but they are best served by other techniques. The present chapter highlights the importance of video in special-purpose language courses at the upper levels.

The more specialized a language course is, the more applications can be found in it for the use of video. For most third-year students, language usage in a particular region and profession is not of prime importance. Rather, the goal is to learn the fundamentals of the language and to assimilate basic vocabulary. But what about students enrolled in courses on Spanish for agricultural purposes, business German, and advanced French phonetics? These students need more than Cervantes, Goethe, and Molière interspersed with *El País, Die Zeit,* and *Le Monde.* Once the curriculum shifts its concentration from the principles of the language conceived as a single broad and long-lived phenomenon to actual communication with real people living in a particular region today, the importance of broadly exemplifying the spoken language in context increases. Because the living language is the material on which the course must be built, it is imperative to give students constant access to today's speakers of the language. There are two ways to provide this access: presence in the foreign culture and large doses of video.

The effectiveness of video in filling this role is seen perhaps most clearly in the case of phonetics courses. I do not refer to the introductory pronunciation course in which students strain to produce a French **u** or a Spanish **r,** but rather to the advanced courses in which students learn to distinguish among speech patterns and accents. In the past, such courses have remained heavily dependent on the teacher's ability to mimic the sounds of regional or class groups or on radio recordings that provided invisible but nevertheless useful native-speaker variations. With television, however, and especially with the development of regional television stations even in the most centralized countries, we discover a new opening onto the everyday world. A broad array of individuals, situations, and language varieties becomes accessible to the advanced classroom. Moreover, this language is no longer disembodied. With the help of video, phonetics can move from its traditional oral/aural presentation to a whole-body performance. As kinesics theoreticians such as Ray L. Birdwhistell and Laurence Wylie have shown, language is never solely a matter of sound.[2] Not only is much communicated by the body, but an understanding of the linguistic phenomenon depends heavily on our ability to observe the body and its surroundings. We are fortunate that the era of kinesics is also the era of the VCR, with its open invitation to analyze and understand the role of the nonverbal in the overall communication process.

The range of potential phonetics and body-language exercises is impressive. Many appropriate activities simply take the video sound track as a source of authentic speech, subject to the same kind of in-class or preparatory processing that characterized earlier approaches: phonetic transcription, imitation, and so forth. The contextual qualities of video, however, offer new and interesting alternatives as well. For example, with a series of short speeches taken from news interviews, documentaries, or narrative fiction, students can complete a sequence of exercises as follows:

1. With the sound track alone, have students develop a police artist's sketch of the speaker, drawing on content, accent, intonation, and any other clues they can locate. Have them describe not only the speaker's background, physical aspect, and body language, but his or her class, age, family position, and other pertinent qualities. Ask them to describe the type of visual background they expect to see in the video sequence. Then play the image so that they can check their conclusions.

2. Using the image alone, have students conjecture about the type of speech they might find on the sound track. What set of phonemes do they expect? How will the language differ from the standard radio announcer's language? What type of sentence construction fits this individual? Will there be major ellipses, nonstandard vocabulary, and other individual characteristics? Does the sound track bear out their expectations?

3. Have students match the sound tracks to the image sequences.

These exercises are particularly well suited for group work. Of course, the exercises alone are only half the story. The discussion they invite and the intelligent commentary of a sensitive, well-trained instructor are all-important. Taken together, preparatory work on the video and in-class follow-up are sure to increase students' sensitivity to the broad complex of concerns at work in oral expression. Even though they may not be accepted as native speakers, students who participate regularly in this type of exercise will soon surpass many native speakers in their ability to analyze an individual's background.

Like phonetics courses, translation courses receive a welcome impetus for oral expression from the video medium. In the distant past, translation courses were restricted to professional schools and were of two well-differentiated types, according to the kind of material translated. If the material was oral, the activity was called *interpreting,* and the emphasis was on speed, as in the ultimate accolade, *simultaneous.* If the material was written, emphasis was on accuracy and style, in accordance with a centuries-old scholarly tradition. Video invites a combination of the two types of translation: the care, patience, and accuracy of written translation coupled with the liveliness and contemporaneity of oral interpreting. To be sure, written texts will continue to be studied and carefully translated, just as a few elite schools around the world will concentrate on simultaneous translation. However, with the introduction of video into college translation courses, an increasing sensitivity to the spoken language will be assured.

This shift in emphasis to oral production will complement students' knowledge of the written language. For example, consider the documents that students consistently manipulate in a course on commercial and technical translation: the written business documents of the country in question. As international businesspeople know, neither the business letter nor the monthly bill lies at the heart of the Mediterranean business world. As important as written documents may be for recording transactions, they accomplish little more than that in much of the traditional world with which we are concerned. From business meetings held over Turkish coffee in the East to contracts signed around a bottle of wine in the West, the **mare nostrum** has its own approach to commercial transactions.

I do not suggest that language courses should first and foremost become practical treatises on how to conduct business on foreign soil. However, if our goal is to prepare students to understand foreign discourse, foreign communication patterns, and foreign transactions, then we should stop limiting students to the written word. On a more practical level, students who can write flawless business letters often have no idea how to cash a check abroad. By increasing students' exposure to aural input in its complete cultural context, we surely broaden their experience and increase their chances of actually using the vocabulary, structures, and cultural knowledge that we labor so hard to teach them. In other words, aural video materials do not simply replicate in sound what the written

Authentic videos specifically made to educate the public often present cultural information in a particularly clear fashion. *La Main dans le sac* is a documentary produced by the Centre National de Documentation Pédagogique to dramatize the entire legal process.

word provides in script. Instead, they carry courses into new areas where the written word rarely ventures and the notion of translation has not been seen before.

For example, more and more language departments are responding to the needs of business schools and law schools by offering courses in business language or including major legal components in other courses. Budding international lawyers and businesspersons thus absorb the terminology of an important but difficult profession. They might learn the difference between a **cour de cassation** and a **cour d'appel,** between a **juge d'instruction** and a **juge de paix.** They know what kind of sentence to expect from what kind of trial, maybe even what kind of paperwork corresponds to what kind of court. Yet by and large they have no idea what the entire process looks like. What does a judge look like? How does a lawyer dress? How is the courtroom arranged? Who is present? What can someone accused of petty theft expect in terms of preliminary procedures and jail cells? Although instructors should not be expected to exemplify or illustrate every circumstance, it would be nice, for example, if bilingual policemen knew what a Spanish one-way-street sign looks like in Spain and in Mexico, as well as knowing the penalty for driving down a one-way street the wrong way.

We are fortunate to have available an increasing number of video materials that facilitate a broad view of the legal system and other cultural subsystems. In France, the Centre National de Documentation Pédagogique has developed, under the direction of Michèle Cohen, a series of video programs on legal matters, designed for general public enlightenment. Many of these programs are fully appropriate for teaching at the upper language level in American schools. For example, *Connaître ses droits* combines four separate consumer education films, each composed of an illustrative sketch and an interview with a specialist. The subjects covered are nonprofit organizations, inheritance law, purchase of property, and theft insurance. *Le Casse de Clamart* presents a fictitious crime and follows the criminal court procedure through sentencing. A thief is shown breaking into a suburban house; a neighbor sees him and gets his license plate number. An accomplice tries to sell the stolen camera equipment; eventually, the burglar is caught and held for a trial, which we follow procedure by procedure. *La Main dans le sac* follows the same path, reconstituting a petty theft and the legal and judicial proceedings that follow.

La Main dans le sac is the subject of a book-length study on video pedagogy that provides a particularly good place to start using video in a course on legal French or business French.[3] In one section of the book, for example, Carmen Compte suggests providing a series of sentences transcribed from the dialogue (pp. 79–80). Students work with these sentences in many different ways, first attributing them to the appropriate characters, then locating them within the story, and finally explaining their importance within the judicial procedure. Lioudmilla Makarova points out the value of having students reconstitute the story in differing styles, tenses, and persons: as a police report or newspaper story, as a letter from a lawyer or inmate, as a report to the drug brigade or a request for the expert opinion of a psychotherapist (p. 101). To these examples might be added a set of oral narrations: the report of the victim to her husband or children, the gossip of an eyewitness or a neighbor of the criminal, a television news report or editorial commentary. I would not be able to resist getting my students to play roles, at first for the action depicted in *La Main dans le sac* and then, still in character, for other judicial situations. Aiming more directly at the legal language, Odile Challe suggests diverse methods of using *La Main dans le sac* to develop students' understanding of the French legal system and its corresponding vocabulary (pp. 154ff).

The practical nature of most business language courses makes them a natural place to introduce video materials. Students in these courses need to know not only how important words are pronounced and in what situation they are used but also what the objects and institutions referred to look like. It is one thing to talk about the stock market or currency fluctuations but another to have an audiovisual sense of how such operations actually take place and are discussed. Programs like *Monnaie et crédit* take students inside the financial institutions in question, giving them a realistic representation, both auditory and visual, of the entire process. Business German students can rapidly gain a picture of the German business world from *ABC der Wirtschaft*.

Audiovisual reinforcement assures greater recall of cultural and linguistic facts. The all-important sensation of comfort and control created by familiarity with the full audiovisual context guarantees more rapid progress toward linguistic production. Linguistic knowledge is undoubtedly important in the teaching of language, but we need to remember that courses in business German, Spanish for health professionals, and commercial and technical French translation teach not only language but culture as well. Without adequate stress on the cultural component, courses on business language leave students inadequately prepared to understand the vocabulary they are supposedly assimilating.

In order to increase students' cultural understanding, special-purpose language courses should accompany video work with the related written or printed documents. The following activities can be used as described or with modifications at various points in business language courses or in related units of more general courses:

1. For a general program on a major business or governmental institution, such as *Histoire de la Poste* or *La Communauté européenne dans le monde,* have students read a related magazine or newspaper article beforehand. This combination will result in a double benefit. First, it will introduce students to unfamiliar

vocabulary and spell out acronyms. Second, it will provide a slightly different, more formal, written view of the phenomenon to be observed. This is a particularly desirable introductory activity to any unit because it successfully relates the written and oral language.

2. For a video commercial, use a magazine advertisement for the same product. This activity fosters discussion about the different advertising strategies involved, the targeted public, and the tie-ins between the two campaigns, thus offering ample opportunity to practice a whole range of important vocabulary. In addition, this activity provides a natural lead-in to another production exercise in which the instructor furnishes an advertisement in one of the media and assigns the student to design a corresponding advertisement in the other. Few things seem to energize this generation of students like writing ad copy. Let's take advantage of that fact!

3. When you find a narrative program that suits your needs particularly well, take advantage of its ability to portray in-dividualized characters in order to encourage students to pro-duce documents reflecting each character's traits. These doc-

Familiar items, like this sports lottery ticket from a *Télématin* ad, provide reinforcement for realia-based oral and written exercises.

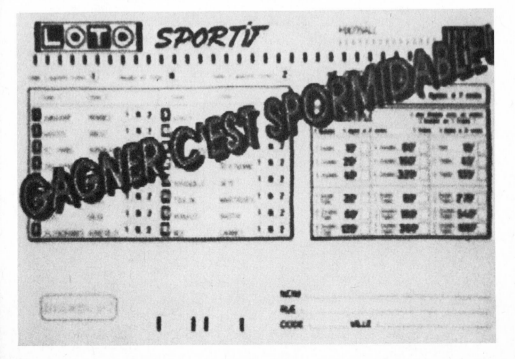

uments should go beyond the tried and true descriptive paragraphs to present the kind of formal portrait required on form after form throughout the lives of people around the world. When you are traveling abroad, bring home some of the following forms for your students to fill out: identity cards, Social Security or passport applications, medical examination papers, driver's license forms, curriculum vitae, voter registration papers, and dozens of other forms that are easily found. If you do not have any forms for the time being, then make up your own or write to a friend abroad for three or four such forms. Using the real thing not only introduces students to far more authentic vocabulary than using homemade versions would, but it also familiarizes students with a country's particular way of imaging and numbering the world. Students are intrigued by all the fine print, the explanations, and the strange administrative ways of asking for perfectly simple information. For this reason, much is to be gained from contrasting, let us say, a West German passport application with its East German, Austrian, and Swiss equivalents, or medical examination papers from diverse Spanish-speaking countries, as well as comparing these with similar U.S. forms.

4. Choose a video program that exemplifies numerous jobs or industries in the countries where your language is spoken. Have students produce a report on one company—such as a description for a stockholders' meeting or stock tender, an accountant's evaluation, an annual report—and a magazine advertisement of an executive position. Once students have looked at the company as an entity, perhaps fictionalizing some aspects, have them change perspective and become job applicants. Each student will then have to develop a personal résumé, write a letter of application, and of course undergo interviews, which will be conducted by other students representing the head of personnel services, the chief of the manufacturing division, the company vice president, and so forth. What is described here is not just a way of making business vocabulary and cultural knowledge concrete through video but a method of energizing and directing student activity through video as well.

5. With a video program providing an in-depth look at a particular business or industry, such as *ABC der Wirtschaft* or *La Soie façonnée à Lyon*, it is best not to stop with the previously described activities. Why not press on to the actual functioning of the business? Students can make up orders, write letters complaining about delays, answer queries, provide self-congratulatory copy for the Chamber of Commerce or local equiv-

alent. There is no limit here to what your own imagination can suggest.

Each of these activities demonstrates two qualities worth striving for in using video, not only in business language courses but in any part of the curriculum in which cultural knowledge and active language production are expected and encouraged. First, the activities should provide entrance not just to the foreign language but also to the culture in which the foreign language is spoken. Authenticity should be paramount in the video and deserves a place of honor in supporting documents as well. Second, activities chosen to support the video should not reinforce the importance of the video but rather serve broader curricular purposes. Video is a fine teaching tool, but integrating video materials into larger educational goals should be of greatest concern. This is the role that the activities suggested here are designed to play. Other approaches will produce similarly valuable results to the extent that they openly strive for these goals.

Choosing programs for use in business language courses is already a pleasure and promises to get better as the years go by. Three categories of programs deserve particular mention. First, a significant number of packaged programs aimed at or appropriate for business language courses are either currently available or in production. Of German origin, but also available with a French sound track, is *ABC der Wirtschaft*. This program is five hours long, occupies thirty-nine separate episodes, and covers topics from banking and insurance to monopolies, embargoes, and the World Bank. A complementary program, not specifically developed for business language courses but particularly appropriate there, is *VELVET*. *VELVET* features native Germans in authentic German situations, although many of the apparently authentic situations are semiscripted, with German actors playing typical roles in the offices and shops of unsuspecting authentic German office personnel and shopkeepers. The result is a carefully directed product that is more accessible to lower-level students than *ABC der Wirtschaft* but still appropriately authentic.

The second category comprises public relations films and video programs produced by companies around the world. Some of these programs are now available to the public. Especially when accompanied by appropriate supporting materials, they provide a fascinating introduction to one range of vocabulary and business practices.

A third source of interesting business materials comes from TV news broadcasts. Programs such as the Antenne 2 *Panorama* and *TV-France Magazine*, which give a monthly summary of important French news, or *Telejournal*, a weekly news program from the BBC, furnish many short features that cover business and related topics. A lab with a good archive of *Panorama* programs encourages a wide variety of independent student activities and reports. For example, students can

TEACHING WITH VIDEO

report individually on features such as the following items (from the 1985–87 period): Bonn meeting of industrialized countries, the EUREKA affair, new French restaurants, art and industry, publicity Oscars, Marcel Dassault, dossier on strikes, success of the Paribas bank. With the experience of a few years' teaching in this manner, instructors will know the *Panorama* backlog well enough to guide their students through the many available documents, thus reinforcing needed review in particular areas.

In the years to come, video pedagogy for special-purpose upper-level courses should develop rapidly and effectively, and not only in high schools and universities. When the world's business schools discover the efficacy of this method, they should make heavy use of video documents for general language and international education purposes. If anything, this trend is likely to spread even more rapidly in the business world itself. The few companies already using video materials from other countries to train their executives going abroad may well be joined by hundreds of others. For the time being, the educational world still has a chance to keep up with, if not surpass, the business world.

Notes

1. See especially the impassioned arguments of Richard Lambert, professor of South Asian Studies at the University of Pennsylvania, who included the strengthening of upper-level language education as one of the basic thrusts in his "Proposal to Create a National Foreign Language Center" (typescript), pp. 16–19. Professor Lambert is director of the recently created National Foreign Language Center, Washington, D.C.

2. For a theoretical introduction to the field of kinesics, see the work of Ray L. Birdwhistell, especially *Introduction to Kinesics: An Annotation System for Analysis of Body Motion and Gesture* (Louisville: University of Louisville Press, 1952), and *Kinesics and Context: Essays on Body Motion Communication* (Philadelphia: University of Pennsylvania Press, 1970). For more practical applications to foreign-language situations, see Laurence Wylie's recent work, for example *Beaux Gestes: A Guide to French Body Talk* (Cambridge, Mass.: Undergraduate Press, 1977).

3. The book, *La Main dans le sac*, is sponsored by the Bureau pour l'Enseignement de la Langue et de la Civilisation françaises à l'étranger (BELC) and written by a team headed by Carmen Compte and including Odile Challe, Chih Min Chen, Michèle Cohen, Marielle Dagher, Christian Dumarty, Maria del Carmen Ferreyra, Lioudmilla Makarova, Pavel Plusa, and Mercedes Solis (Paris: BELC, 1986). See especially the "Approche linguistique" (Lioudmilla Makarova), pp. 84–120; the "Approche par transcriptions comparées" (Maria del Carmen Ferreyra and Mercedes Solis), pp. 131–53; and, for business French, the "Approche fonctionnelle" (Odile Challe), pp. 171ff.

CHAPTER 7
Video in the Civilization Curriculum

What is civilization? Where do we find it? Not so many decades ago, the answers to these questions seemed obvious to everyone: *civilization,* as in *civilized,* as in *Western civilization,* as in *the westward course of civilization.* Not so long ago, to speak of civilization was to refer to Greece and Rome, to the revival of classical learning in the Renaissance, to the growth of the neoclassical style in literature and art, to kings and queens, reigns and revolutions, art and architecture, castles and culture. From Charlemagne to Charles V, from Louis XIV to Mad Ludwig, from Joan of Arc to General de Gaulle, from the palace of Versailles to the Treaty of Versailles, civilization was long a European affair, the fief of the ruling class, the private preserve of those who make the history that goes into the textbooks.

Today the textbooks have changed. Thanks to the "New History" practiced by the *Annales* school, we no longer see history as the sole province of the ruling class and the isolated event. The new interest in daily events and practices has enfranchised the common people, now recognized by many as the vessels of a new and profound civilization. At the same time, it has opened up the field of history to non-European countries. Once restricted to the discipline of anthropology, the study of the world beyond Western civilization has been retrieved by a new anthropological brand of history. Group after group, once banned by an elite notion of civilization, has found a place in the pages of history: women, children, household servants, artisans, retired workers, farmers, immigrants. As history has taken up the provincial, the rural, and the domestic, our very notion of civilization has changed; it is no longer even restricted to the past.

Video is doubly part of this revolution. Not only is television largely responsible for capturing daily life around the nation and the world, thus making the quotidian newly accessible to the historian and the person in the street alike, but video also has the power to recall this daily life, to make it available at any time for study or discussion. Just as historians such as Lefèvre and Bloch, Duby and Braudel—the architects of the new school of history—consistently turned to the seemingly banal records of daily events, such as marriage licenses, sales ledgers, land transfers, deeds, and the like, so video provides us with the daily log of

Recording every poster and sign, video is the ideal medium to convey culture with a little "c". A political poster shows a French working woman's reaction to the prospect of a right wing victory in an upcoming election. (*Télé-douzaine*)

contemporary civilization. Like the New Historians before us, however, we are faced with an embarrassment of riches. The question is not so much *where* to look to find something useful but *which* of the many appropriate programs to choose and *how* to use them. This chapter suggests a few of the most useful strategies and the most successful programs for teaching the new understanding of civilization.

I Witness

What is civilization for you? Is it a list of presidents, a series of census statistics, a table of cultural changes during a particular decade? Or is it the individuals who constitute the culture, along with the social situation specific to them? By and large, these are the poles between which most approaches to civilization oscillate. On one side are individual human beings in all their intriguingly unquantifiable specificity; on the other are the statistics and generalizations that permit us to compare one period or country with another. As I see it, the teaching of civilization is heavily marked by the need to create continuity between these two opposite approaches. When the material presents particular individuals through the case study method, our task is to help students see how that particularity reflects more general concerns and trends. In the more common situation in which the material provides the statistics and the general truths, we labor hard to give our students a more personalized view of the civilization in question.

Video is admirably equipped to carry out the latter function. If the Latin **video** means *I see* and **audio** means *I hear,* then the overall audiovisual complex implies *I witness.* Able to experience culture not only as a statistic but also as living truth, the viewer/auditor truly becomes an *eyewitness.* This is true at every level, as three specific examples will illustrate.

1. The simplest form of video is what we might call the *illustrated list.* A textbook might include a list of French presidents accompanied by their portraits. In the same way, the video program entitled *La Présidence de la République* begins with a voice-over presentation on and picture of each French president in turn. What is gained through the visual approach, even in this elementary form, is a supplement of information and authenticity. The changes in portrait positions, clothing fashions, hair treatment, beards and mustaches, and even facial types are not just window dressing; they are part of civilization itself. They offer students both a supplement of knowledge and a strikingly effective way to help that knowledge stick. Think of American history and the extent to which *images* of George Washington, Abraham Lincoln, Teddy Roosevelt, and John F. Kennedy have marked our sense of history. Students learning about other cultures have an even greater need to *visualize* the past of those cultures.

2. A more complex type of video program might be termed the *exemplified study.* Here, the generalities of cultural analysis are presented along with concrete examples that justify them. Two approaches to this type of program are common. Most historical films are assembled out of archival footage with an explanatory voice-over sound track, as in the medieval trilogy *Beynac, un château au moyen âge, Evocation médiévale: Semur-en-Auxois,* and *Monastères du moyen âge.* In the same way, many documentaries on an entire country use voice-over com-

mentary to justify the joining of otherwise unrelated images in a single program, as in the RTVE documentary, *Venezolanos*. A more creative example can be found in *D'hier à aujourd'hui: La population française*, which intertwines a census report on new trends in the French population with a series of vignettes illustrating the life of a single French family over several generations. Programs like this one invite students both to pay attention to individual cases and to relate them to general trends. Furthermore, these programs have the advantage of providing authentic speech as well as authentic images, whereas the voice-over approach tends to reduce regional and class speech differences to a single common denominator.

3. Still another type of program provides a video case study. With films of this type students enter an era through the eyes of a particular set of people. Students who view *El pueblo sumergido* gain more than book knowledge of Spanish rural reform policies. They see and hear what it was like to live through a period of changing expectations and living conditions. Of course, like the individuals of that era, students may have some difficulty seeing the general forces at work in daily life. The task of helping students concentrate on the movement from particular to general is considerably easier if the selected program deals not just with a single case but with a series of them. From this point of view, *Douze ans après* is exemplary. Each of four women is interviewed twice in this striking program, once in the early 1970s and again in the mid-1980s. The program provides students with extraordinary opportunities to develop an understanding of the changing status of women in French society, because its multiple cases and dual time-levels prevent students from forming simplistic conclusions about Franco-American differences.

All of these approaches offer the student a chance to witness civilization in action, not just as statistic but as living process. They invite students to remain mindful of the fundamental continuity between individual human beings and the general trends that constitute culture.

Strategies for Cultural Awareness

From the lowest level of language teaching to the most advanced civilization course, promoting student awareness of cultural specificity remains an important goal. As we labor to overcome the cultural insularity that often characterizes American life, a variety of different aspects of culture call for our attention. At the simplest level are features of life in another country that are shared by the vast majority of the population. Equally important are unique or local features exhibited only at a special time of the year or in a particular part of the target culture. In addition, historical aspects of the foreign civilization call for increased attention in advanced courses. These three basic approaches to cultural awareness are treated in turn in this section.

The Shared Civilization of Everyday Life

Certainly one of the most exciting aspects of video is the moving picture that it provides of everyday life in another country. Whether the program in question is presented as a detective story, a documentary, a series of interviews, or a public relations program, the creative instructor will always see it also as a cultural document. The background of the detective story constantly reveals local traffic and buildings. The documentary may provide an instructive view of eating and living habits. The interviews furnish information on dress codes and language patterns. The public relations program complements foregrounded information with images of working conditions and statements about cultural priorities. Every authentic video program offers opportunities to notice and discuss the lifestyle and living circumstances of another culture.

Heightening student awareness of cultural difference usually requires more than a simple exercise asking students to list cultural practices different from their American equivalents. At first, students often have a hard time recognizing the particularities of foreign culture because they are so unselfconscious about their own culture. In any course stressing cultural concerns, early lessons are thus well spent sensitizing students both to foreign practices and to their American equivalents. It is perhaps best to point out such practices in passing, during video activities that are not specifically aimed at cultural awareness. Once students have been shown how to look for and recognize the cultural practices that underlie more overt aspects of the video, they will be better able to complete cultural exercises on their own.

These exercises may be extremely varied in nature. As a rule, important cultural practices should be presented not only through video but with the added support of another medium. A preliminary reading passage describing the reasons for or the effects of a particular practice will help students to broaden their understanding of the practice and thus to remember it. Study questions to accompany out-of-class viewing can be extremely helpful in gently guiding students toward a fuller understanding of another culture. By asking students to identify a particular object or to explain a specific action, carefully formulated questions can easily direct attention to important concerns even before these concerns are stressed in class. Exercises that focus specifically on cultural aspects are of course central to the heightening of cultural awareness, but the opportunity to use sentences related to cultural concerns within exercises primarily directed at grammar or vocabulary should not be neglected.

Because students can benefit from the eye of an expert on the foreign culture, in-class activities will appropriately depend heavily on information provided by the teacher, either orally or through handouts related to the video material. Once students have begun to understand particular cultural differences, however, it is important to provide them with an opportunity to practice their new knowledge. Students who have viewed *El pueblo sumergido*, one of the episodes of *Ein kurzes Leben lang*, or *D'hier à aujourd'hui: La population française* will benefit from an activity that requires them to reveal a personal understanding of the target culture. Students can be asked to respond as characters in the video program might, answering questions formulated by the teacher or other students. This activity will take on greater realism if the questions are asked from the point of view of a fictional character created by the class and represented by different students in turn. This fictional character should be appropriate to the circumstances of the video used. For *El pueblo sumergido* it might be a sociologist or a social worker. *Ein kurzes Leben lang* might call for a visitor from out of town or a neighbor of the Kern family. For *D'hier à aujourd'hui: La population française,* questions might be asked by the census official depicted in the film or an absent relative of the Le Guennec family.

The important thing is to challenge students who have seen how a foreign culture works to begin thinking like the members of that culture. This process can involve activities as simple as shaking hands in imitation of the characters in a French program, or it can be expanded to the level of complex skits, such as those that might be produced by students who have observed Latin American ethnology in the RTVE documentary *Quechuas, Huicholes y Panameños*. With imaginative instruction and access to authentic video, students will soon become far more sophisticated in their ability to understand foreign cultures.

The Broader Culture: Groups, Regions, Holidays

One of the greatest problems in teaching civilization, at whatever level, is to establish an appropriate balance between the dominant culture and the broader culture. Whereas certain habits may be thought of as dominating a particular culture, these practices are by no means the only ones practiced within the culture. Understanding of the broader culture depends on attention to the activities characteristic of a particular population, space, or time. One of the best ways to assure the necessary emphasis on the broader culture is through careful program selection. Of the Spanish-speaking programs available, by far the majority concentrate on Spain. These may be usefully complemented by *Venezolanos, Un paseo por Hispanoamérica* or *Quechuas, Huicholes y Panameños*. Similarly, the many programs on France need to be balanced by programs on Canada or other Francophone countries. Programs from Austrian television can serve the same purpose for the German-speaking world.

The broadened view of a culture also includes minority groups and widely differing regions within a country. For lower-level students of French, stress on the dominant culture seems perfectly appropriate; advanced civilization students, however, are well served by programs that broaden their view of French culture. Typical programs stress the traditional Catholic population; programs like *Le Calife d'Argenteuil, Touche pas à mon pote, Femmes immigrées,* and *Radio Beur* provide an opportunity to highlight the culture of recent immigrant populations. Many programs take Paris as representative of the whole of France; films like *Regain, Vaches bien ordonnées,* and *La Production laitière* make it possible to highlight life in rural France. Most programs concentrate on French men; only with the help of programs like *Delphine Delamare, Sur l'éducation des filles, Douze ans après,* and *Vivre femme* will students become sensitive to the quite different lives of French women. In each target culture, alternate programs like these must be found if we are to avoid easy oversimplifications about the population as a whole.

In order to capitalize on the variety of costumes and customs around the country and throughout the year, instructors might encourage students to make regular additions to a cultural map and a cultural calendar kept in the course notebook. This approach naturally leads to exercises in which students identify the limits of particular cultural phenomena. Whereas early exercises might have concentrated on the difference between U.S. culture and the target culture, later exercises might require students to identify the limits of a foreign practice. Apropos of specific actions, postures, or statements, students might be asked whether the same practice would be followed by (a) someone of the opposite sex, (b) a person from a different age group, (c) an inhabitant of a different region, (d) an individual with a different ethnic background, (e) a member of another class. In dealing with architecture, urban design, rural land use, or the general look of the countryside, more advanced students can be asked to identify the region in which they might expect to find a particular feature and the aesthetic or economic role it plays. By separating the target culture into a series of subcultures, this method helps students to become sensitive to important differences *within* the culture as well as *between* cultures.

Historical Perspectives

Sensitivity to variations within a culture is essential to an understanding of political concerns and social unrest. It is also fundamental to comprehension of cultural history. Neophytes often assume that practices encountered in another country are the mark of some fundamental and eternal difference between populations and cultures. Not recognizing that cultural practices change from decade to decade or from century to century, beginners attribute them instead to some undefinable racial or cultural imperative. Video can help students mature in their understanding of cultural differences. By revealing historical differences in the cultural practices of a single country, authentic foreign video or carefully made reconstructions reveal the specificity of individual cultures.

For some eras, the most appropriate programs are simply recent documentaries on past periods. The French Middle Ages take on a new material existence when exemplified by *Beynac, un château au moyen âge, Evocation médiévale: Semur-en-Auxois* or *Monastères du moyen âge*. In other cases, students will grow fastest in their historical understanding of culture when they can work with video materials matched to previously studied literary texts. Through programs like *Montaigne dans son labyrinthe, Les Chemins de la sérénité: Jean-Jacques Rousseau, Victor Hugo et la révolution,* or video versions of Maupassant short stories, past eras of French culture can be made to come alive, especially for students familiar with the language and literature of the era in question. In fact, the experience of studying culture through video can make the study of literature more culturally rewarding as well. Students accustomed to viewing video versions of literary texts can easily imagine the visual and spatial dimensions of the literary texts they are reading. Students who have seen *Johann Wolfgang von Goethe* are more likely to visualize characters in period dress than in modern American dress when reading Goethe's novels.

The study of contemporary civilization derives perhaps the most benefit from the use of video materials. Most video programs reveal a recent version of the culture, thus favoring the study of current practices. This is especially important with younger students, who often are impatient with images that they deem old-fashioned. In sensitizing students to current cultural concerns, the use of other media to complement television is especially important. For example, students might be asked to analyze a video program on the basis of a preliminary reading from a news magazine. Does the video program demonstrate or disagree with the cultural thesis developed in the article? Which parts of the program support the thesis? Which parts contradict it?

This approach can be used especially fruitfully with survey information about the target country. With a geographically oriented program, students might read a poll about preferred vacation spots and then answer questions regarding the relationship between the poll and the video. With a program highlighting the life of a specific family, like *Ein kurzes Leben lang* or *D'hier à aujourd'hui: La population française,* students might be given information about family organization, income, opinions, and so forth. As they answer questions about the video, they are constantly encouraged to compare the family in the film with national norms and values and thus discouraged from reaching too-easy conclusions about the representativeness of the family. With little difficulty, instructors will find appropriate newspaper articles, magazine features, or published statistics that help to contextualize case study video programs. Conversely, enterprising teachers will discover in the print medium appropriate case studies or local stories to complement video programs that are too broad or general to furnish the individual note on which students of all ages thrive.

Today's Civilization, Tomorrow's News

The more we are concerned with truly contemporary civilization, the more we must abandon the carefully planned and produced program in favor of news reports, fragments of history on the move, civilization in the making. Because of its topical and episodic nature, the news presents a special challenge for the video-conscious instructor. Unlike programs used yearly for language instruction, the news involves throwaway preparation—development of strategies for the teaching of this week's news that will no longer be applicable at a later date. Furthermore, using news reduces to nearly nothing the time available to prepare appropriate materials. In spite of these problems, however, the news is an attractive teaching tool. It has all the qualities of the live target. You may not hit it as often as the stationary one, but you will come back again and again to take a shot at it, because its constant, unpredictable movements suggest that it has a life of its own.

International video news is available in a variety of formats. For the purposes of language and civilization teachers, there are four major sources.

1. **Satellite Transmission of Live News Programming.** In the United States, this source is largely limited to broadcasts in Spanish (SIN), Russian (Vremya), and French (Canadian), though in the future a far greater range of news programs will certainly become available. Indeed, the SCOLA network,

directed by Father Lee Lubbers of Creighton University, already provides access to retransmitted programs from numerous national systems.

2. **Satellite Transmission of Edited News Programming.** Live programming often loses in comprehensibility what it gains in authenticity. When the news your students are watching is the same as that aimed at foreign nationals, there will be serious comprehension problems. The University of Maryland–Baltimore County solves this problem by transmitting for satellite reception a carefully constituted digest of French news from the preceding month, prepared by Antenne 2 in France. This solution retains the topical interest of news programs, but it also benefits from a purposeful choice of items most likely to appeal to an American audience interested in contemporary French civilization but not necessarily fluent in French.[1] Many other local projects to distribute foreign programming by satellite are now under development.

3. **Videocassette Distribution of Edited Current News Programming.** Cassette distribution simplifies reception and copyright problems, while offering the educational community access to a growing archive of news programs. French news selections on cassette are now widely available, on a monthly basis in the *Panorama* series, twice a month in the *France-Panorama* series. German and Spanish news materials are currently represented only by *Telejournal,* a BBC program now available in the United States. Each week throughout the academic year, *Telejournal* provides an edited version, with an English-language introduction, of a news broadcast in French, German, or Spanish.

4. **Videocassette or Videodisc Distribution of Graded Selections from Previous News Programs.** This type of source is primarily represented by *Télé-douzaine* and *Nachrichten I,* both accompanied by a simplified second sound track and available on videodisc as well as cassette. These programs provide well-chosen compilations from previous news programs and present an especially appropriate way to initiate students into the news as an important source of information about contemporary civilization. (*See Chapter 4 for specific suggestions of ways to use edited news programs in lower-level language teaching.*)

Each of these sources plays its own special role in a properly constituted civilization program.

For students who already possess a basic understanding of another culture and language, news programs have a number of special advantages

News programs provide two major types of material: topical coverage of the day's events, as in this German *Telejournal* segment, and short feature stories like this *Télématin* report on a French village split between two **départements.**

and drawbacks. Warned about the potential difficulties, however, teachers can easily stress the virtues while minimizing the problems. Three areas in particular deserve some forethought: motivation, language, and culture.

One of the strongest arguments in favor of using the news in civilization courses is its energizing potential. Whether or not it is live, the news retains the value of the new. Students are often unexpectedly fascinated by reports that might not interest them at all in English. We pay for this motivating factor, since the very newness of the news makes it hard to prepare for and thus hard to integrate into an overall curriculum. Nevertheless, solutions do exist. The most obvious is to simulate newness, as with the news-on-cassette system of *Telejournal* and *Panorama.* Students will still be energized by the newness of the material, but you will have the time to prepare supporting materials.

With direct satellite reception the problem is more difficult but not unresolvable. In order to gain maximum value from directly transmitted news, however, you must remember that *you* are the boss, not the news announcer. Learn to predict the news by referring to your own knowledge of current events. Before viewing, choose the areas you want your students to concentrate on. Do not expect them to understand political, economic, and cultural news immediately; instead, prepare them each week for a different area. Preparation might include the traditional vocabulary list, but you will achieve greater success with a parallel reading, one that treats current events from the point of view stressed that week. The reading provides vocabulary in context and fosters awareness of the type of problem likely to be discussed in the news. Armed with a preliminary reading and aware of the general concern of the news broadcast, students are better prepared for appropriate follow-up activities. These activities may involve classroom discussion (including indirect explanation of difficult areas), another reading chosen for its connection to the broadcast, or a project that requires research either in the library or simply among the classroom magazine collection. Another activity involves comparing U.S. and foreign viewpoints on the same news.

The range of language typically employed in a newscast represents another major advantage. Students pick up useful terms in context, the kind of terms that are necessary for treating contemporary concerns of all sorts. This vocabulary stretches far beyond traditional vocabulary. One of the most important contributions of the news is its ability to help us sense a culture from within and thus understand what kind of knowledge is taken for granted. Symbolic of this important function is the acronym. What acronyms are used in the news? What organizations, practices, or diseases are deemed so familiar to viewers that they do not have to be spelled out? This assumption of familiarity is a marker of cultural specificity that a serious civilization course cannot afford to ignore.

Ironically, this is where the advantage of newscasts stops and the problems start. It is one thing to accept the theoretical importance of acronyms, code words, and proper nouns and quite another to assure full understanding on the part of students. An unadulterated European news item on the European Economic Community (EEC in English, CEE in French, EWG in German) is sure to drive the basic civilization student mad, with its multiple acronyms, its code words, its regular use of names derived from different national traditions but all pronounced with the same Belgian or Austrian accent. The best solution is to begin by accentuating the positive. What *did* students understand? How can you expand that understanding? Stress the important terms, the ones that are sure to receive reinforcement in succeeding weeks. Have students keep an alphabetical culture log in which they enter the names of important organizations and individuals, along with their acronyms or well-known nicknames. Above all, assume that the vocabulary of every newscast will be a problem for your students, even if it is not for you. Remember that you have absorbed vast amounts of cultural knowledge that your students do not yet have. Unless you can look beyond your own knowledge of the target culture, you will not be able to locate problems and remedy them.

Central to news programs is, of course, the news. Language instructors concentrate on these programs in part because they believe that current events have something to teach students about other countries. Instruction comes not just from the events themselves but also from the way in which they are reported and the reactions that they elicit. This important quality of the news constitutes a dangerous trap, however. In spite of its name, the news is not only the news: it is also fascinating footage from the target culture, along with captivating speech. The news announcer would like the viewer/listener to think that what is being viewed is important primarily because of its news value. Refuse to accept the announcer's approach as the only one available. Ask students about the background, the clothing, the choice of words, the difference in speech between the police and the suspect. Have them forget about the news for a minute and locate in the image three typically Italian practices and explain when and how they became part of Italian culture. Have them demonstrate the extent to which a particular report depends on Spanish legal practices. Ask students to show how the same episode might have been reported from the point of view of the American legal system. In short, do not let the news become reduced to just news; the fact that particular words and images contain a newsworthy item should not insulate those words and images from a different reading. Be creative and, above all, do not succumb to the very real temptation to let the news run your class.

Finally, remember that today's news will be tomorrow's history. One of the advantages of buying the news on cassette, rather than simply watching a broadcast, is that you can legally keep the program indefinitely. Now that the fifties and sixties are history and regularly enter into civilization courses, don't you wish that somebody had been archiving foreign news programs for posterity? Think of how a news archive might change the teaching of recent civilization. Start your archive now and you will be using it yourself in less than a decade.

Video as Civilization

Throughout this book I have suggested ways in which television programs can serve purposes that are not necessarily the ones for which they were intended. The time has come to recognize that the original purpose of television programs may indeed have a place in the curriculum. What kinds of programs are broadcast by other national television systems? Who finances them? When are they scheduled? What technical resources are available? What editorial function is served? Who makes the decisions? How many people watch which programs with what attitude? These and dozens of other questions come to mind when one considers that the media make up a major part of the modern world and thus of contemporary civilization.

Given the relative unavailability of authentic foreign broadcast television programs in their original form, it is not easy to implement a successful television section in a contemporary civilization course, let alone a full-blown course on a national television system.[2] Although several distributors include in their catalogues programs that originated on foreign television, many of these programs have been repackaged with new introductions or other disguises, thus dissimulating the original format. Even an unadulterated program rarely gives any indication of where it originated, when it was broadcast, and so forth.

The solution to this problem lies in creative use of print materials. What is our goal in studying video as civilization? Surely it is to consider how another country makes television programs and also how those programs fit into the culture as a whole. This kind of knowledge can never be gained solely from the programs themselves; it always requires a close look at the culture's own discourse about its television programming. By far the best source of such discourse is the printed guide to television programming, the foreign equivalent of our *TV Guide*. Even the worst of these guides provides precious information on types and time of programming, on the relation between the local television system and other systems (notably the American), and on the attitude of the audience toward various categories of programming, as well as on the type of print advertising aimed at television viewers. Do you want your students to understand France's peculiar combination of popular culture and philosophical intellectualism? Have them work with the extraordinarily well-written and well-produced television magazine *Télérama,* as well as with the more popular *Téléstar* or *Télé 7 jours.* The types of article, the nature of the information provided, the complexity of the film analyses, the kind of advertisements accompanying the text—all these things speak loudly and clearly about a culture. Even if you do not plan a separate unit on the media, you may want to make use of local television guides: they are truly gold mines of useful material.

Once students have taken an interest in foreign video programming, they will continue making comparisons with American television. This approach has exciting possibilities, but discussion can easily become bogged down if students are prepared to contribute nothing more than their first impressions. If you have never done so, you may wish to do some reading on television yourself to help you guide students' responses.[3] Controlled comparisons are especially useful. For example, have teams of students compare a selection of German-language newscasts with their American equivalents. Consider variables of time of day, day of week, station, and so forth. This exercise is even more valuable if you can include a comparison of newspaper reports for the same day. Having to distinguish between different approaches within the same country as well as between countries keeps students from jumping to conclusions. Here again, the television viewing guide is an essential support mechanism, providing a ready source of vocabulary as well as a clear commentary on cultural attitudes toward television in general and different types of programs in particular.

During the fifties and sixties, language and literature departments around the country added civilization courses to their rosters. During the seventies and eighties, special courses on business language and foreign cinema began to flourish. In the nineties, the popular new course may be the foreign media course; such courses are already being offered at Clark University, Middlebury College, and the University of Iowa. There is so much to be gained at every level through study of the foreign media that more such courses are bound to spring up as soon as the requisite materials become available. Even now, much is possible.

Notes

1. In 1987–88, *France-TV Magazine* was transmitted on the first Wednesday of each school month at 1:00 P.M. eastern time on Westar 4–99 degrees, Transponder 10D, Channel 19 (4080 MHz). According to special arrangement with Antenne 2, copies of *France-TV Magazine* may be freely made and retained until May 31 of the school year following the original transmission. For further information, contact *France-TV Magazine*, AC IV, Rm. 214, University of Maryland-Baltimore County, Baltimore, Md. 21228-5398; tel. 301/455-2963.

2. Nevertheless, such courses are beginning to pop up, especially in institutions that are members of the Project for International Communication Studies (PICS) consortium. Courses entirely devoted to French television, for example, have been taught at the University of Iowa by Janet Altman and Jim Pusack, at Middlebury College by François Mariet, and at Clark University by Marcia Butzel and Phil Rosen.

3. For beginners, I recommend Horace Newcomb, *Television: The Critical View*, 4th ed. (New York: Oxford University Press, 1987) and Robert C. Allen, ed., *Channels of Discourse* (Chapel Hill: University of North Carolina Press, 1987). The latter volume contains a bibliography.

CHAPTER 8
Video Outside the Classroom

As we are all aware, learning takes place in many different situations. Students learn in the classroom and from their assigned homework, but they also learn from visiting lecturers, foreign films, language-house programs, foreign-language radio stations, and myriad other informal activities. Some of these activities cannot be programmed, but others can be carefully planned. This chapter takes an informed look around the campus and the town in order to discover the many ways in which international video can serve as a catalyst for learning, even far from the classroom. It begins, however, close to home.

The Language Laboratory

Whether it is called Learning Laboratory or Language Media Center, whether it is just a cart in a closet or an entire building, a permanent facility independent of the classroom can play an important role in video pedagogy. One of video's most important virtues lies in its ability to put students at ease. How can its magic possibly work under the watchful eye of the instructor? Properly configured and scheduled, the language lab provides an environment in which students can take full advantage of video's potential. Equipping a lab for video work requires careful planning, however.[1] Making the right decisions depends not only on knowing how students will use the video material but also on understanding how students react to video.

In nearly every school or university, three different types of viewing must be planned for: individual viewing, group viewing, and small-group viewing.

Individual Viewing

Individual viewing may take place in a wide variety of circumstances, even in institutions with only a single VCR. It can include assigned homework, drop-in self-enrichment viewing, faculty previewing or independent study, and special projects such as those for gifted students, those for fourth-year students in high schools that offer only three years of language study, and term papers in civilization courses. Little special preparation is needed for this kind of work, unless computer-controlled video is involved. Any VCR in the lab will suffice for single individual viewing, as long as the problem of isolation has been solved, either by partitions or a headset. Individual usage that is not class-related can be maximized in a number of ways, almost all of which involve advertising the video wares available in the lab and their potential benefits. Put a monitor outside the lab and show a new video each week, with a poster inviting students to request the tapes they would like to see. Post a list of available programs and be sure to note which ones are accompanied by transcripts, exercises, and other ancillary materials. Send out a circular to faculty members announcing the availability not only of new materials in their fields but also of materials in related fields for which students may need language instruction. At the University of Iowa, we regularly use video materials to help train faculty members going abroad for research or exchange-teaching purposes. Individual viewing will take place more often, of course, in situations where students have access to home or dorm VCRs and can check out videotapes from the lab. With video costs plummeting, a videotape exchange program cannot be too far away.

Group Viewing

Group viewing is a different story. Depending on the size of the group involved, a mobile cart equipped with a VCR and monitor may or may not suffice. If a choice must be made, choose the cart system over a fixed installation. A mobile setup may be needed when a classroom never before scheduled for a language course must be used or when two important video-supported lectures are set for the same time slot. With the independence provided by properly equipped carts, you can easily interchange a multistandard and a single-standard setup or replace a faulty system with one that is working. You will have maximum flexibility in scheduling individual as well as group viewing, since the cart setup can be shared by both, as long as you are using hip-height rather than shoulder-height carts. You will be free to configure the classroom or the lab in any way desired: with everyone in the room watching video, a small group working on video, or a single individual viewing video in the corner. If you must show video to groups too large for a single monitor, then consider purchasing projection video equipment. This solution retains the flexibility of the cart system, as long as you are using a mobile projection video, but facilitates showings to large groups.

Strategies for maximizing group viewing are by and large quite familiar to instructors and language lab directors alike, since the film medium has for decades been available for foreign-language group viewing. Video programs, however, are shorter, more varied, and potentially more numerous than films. They can thus be combined in many more ways. For example, a foreign advertisement week can be sponsored, with collages of magazine ads for posters and a campaign to vote on the best commercial as part of the showing. A women's video festival can be organized, perhaps cosponsored by a local women's group. Students can make video ads for the local Oktoberfest, Carnival, or Mardi Gras to be shown in language classes and on public-access TV. Weekly showings of video programs in which the language, level, and theme change regularly can be set up.[2] Use your imagination. But don't count on one person's imagination alone. Invite colleagues and students to organize video festivals or to use video showings as part of larger events. Remember that departments other than language departments may have more than a passing interest in such activities.

Small-Group Viewing

Common Western languages have accustomed us to think in terms of the singular and the plural: individual and group viewing. With video, however, a third number concept is necessary, for many of video's most characteristic qualities appear only in the context of small-group viewing. Alone or in a large group, the video spectator remains a fairly passive consumer. Even when this spectator shows a reaction, it is typically directed straight back at the screen—for example, as laughter. This kind of one-on-one viewing has its virtues, especially when the student has a video workbook or other set of exercises to interact with. Video fully fulfills its potential, however, only when it serves as a catalyst for additional activity. We know this from observing the home viewing situation. When our children are lost in a trance while watching their favorite TV programs, only one kind of learning takes place. When they interact with those around them, however, the road is opened to new kinds of learning. As educators have been insisting for decades, only through this type of interaction can television become a positive force in society. The same logic prevails with international video. Students should not be limited to learning from the image and sound only. Under the right conditions, video induces interaction among spectators and expands the learning process. (*See Chapter 10 for examples of language lab configurations particularly conducive to such small-group interaction.*)

Perhaps the best encouragement for increased small-group viewing comes from a friendly staff, aware of who is in what booth and always ready to suggest the formation of a small group. Scheduling can also help. Instead of the tried and true sign-up sheets with room for one name per slot, leave room for the names of six students, or whatever number of students the cubicle or area will accommodate. This will encourage students to form their own viewing groups or to sign up for viewing with a desirable companion. With proper facilities, instructors should also be encouraged to make small-group project assignments, such as reports, term papers, pastiches, and the like. Not every group will do the same amount of talking in the target language, but experience suggests that the better the students and the greater their commitment to language learning and their feeling of comfort in the language lab, the more likely they are to employ the target language for discussion. Since small-group viewing is still new, we do not yet have all the answers about how to use it properly. It is, however, the strategy of the future.

Video Around the Campus

Is there room for international video on your campus or in your school? You may not know until you have tried. This section suggests some of the many ways in which foreign video programs can contribute to an overall educational experience. Remember, though, that successful ideas must grow out of local situations, concerns, and possibilities. The most important resources are your own faculty and students, along with the local community. During the fifties and sixties, the demand for slide presentations by individuals returning from abroad was great. Times have changed and so has technology. As colleagues and students acquire VCRs and video cameras, opportunities arise for video presentations in an increasing number of educational arenas.

The campus language house, for example, is a natural place for international video programs. If the language house has a VCR and monitor, preferably of the multistandard type, and if the language lab can make the cassettes available, the language house can become an international audiovisual center. Successful events always require the knowledge and planning of energetic people. Video programs must be chosen and sequenced, posters must be designed and distributed, and an audience must be assured. At the University of Iowa we have addressed these concerns in a number of ways. In one case, a former language-house counselor, who had taken a course on French television, was asked to run a series of Sunday afternoon programs of French video. Starting with *Dallas* in French and working toward more substantial fare, this organizer chose, introduced, and commented on programs with which she was already familiar. The approach worked well because it provided just the right amount of planning. The tapes were not expected to show themselves, nor was some lecturer forced on the students. They laughed and screamed, ate and drank, wandered in and out according to their needs and desires. A similar approach was used for German video. In both cases, entertainment was the overt goal, not education. Students are, of course, sophisticated enough to know that more is involved, but they appreciate a chance to relax in another language. Video is especially good at inviting them to do so.

Language tables are another appropriate place for international video. One of the common problems of language tables is a lack of shared interests among the diverse individuals present. Showing a recent newscast or a controversial short program at the very beginning of the meal can help solve this problem. The program should last no more than fifteen minutes, so as not simply to substitute viewing for speaking. This approach can serve to bring together those who are interested in a particular culture or language and to provide them with an appropriate conversation topic. Video has a service to perform almost any time that students of a foreign language or culture are gathered together. Even if the gathering is just a class party or holiday celebration, check out the appropriate tapes. Where photographs, slides, film strips, records, or tapes once were used, the videotape now finds its place, providing con-textualized authentic language and inviting viewers to continue the con-versation in the same language.

Students who are planning trips abroad or who have just come from abroad constitute a group with special video potential. Does your school participate in a program abroad? What better preparation for students' arrival in another country than videotapes provided by the foreign hosts, introducing major aspects of the country, city, school, and area where the students will be studying. A surprising number of purposes can be fulfilled by an evening viewing of such programs: not just recruitment or dissemination of knowledge but language practice, group solidarity, and creation of a productive atmosphere as well. Videotapes can play a similar role upon the group's return. Whether they consist of homemade video or familiar television programming, videotapes can bring the group back together for useful reinforcement of lessons learned abroad.

Students are not the only ones who can benefit from video sessions. Two specific faculty uses of video also come to mind. Medical doctors have to participate in professional seminars to keep their credentials up to date. A similar requirement is growing more common in the educational field. Even where no such requirement exists, however, the importance of keeping language and cultural knowledge current is widely recognized. Video offers a special potential for this kind of professional seminar, for it provides not only recent cultural material but also the authentic language that logically goes along with it. For many faculty members, the monthly news compilation will serve as a perfect excuse for getting together socially and talking about current events from abroad.

For other faculty members—perhaps heading for Kenya for political science research, or Korea for sociological work, or Japan on an exchange professorship—foreign languages are intimidating. They may believe they read the language well enough to get by in their research but may worry about aural comprehension. How about some videotapes in Swahili, Korean, or Japanese?[5] Working at their own pace, at a level of their own choosing, they can attune their ears in the months preceding their departure. In decades to come, use of videotapes will become a major method for working on the less-taught languages as well as for brushing up on the more common ones.

Video Beyond the Campus

To a striking extent, education in the United States has been conceived as an institutional affair: grammar school, junior high, high school, college, and so it ends. To be sure, there are exceptions, from adult education and professional refresher courses to educational TV and private language schools. By and large, however, it is assumed that education takes place during the school years. This attitude is particularly detrimental to the language-learning process. Students who complete four years of language study in college are typically able to communicate effectively at a limited level in the target language, but they clearly need further training in order to reach the level of fluency and expertise necessary for conducting business affairs in a second or third language or for following the current affairs of another country.[4] International video programs will not by themselves solve this problem, but they do have the independence, authenticity, and topicality needed to engender a new effort in the area of **formation continue,** as the French call their national system of business-related adult education. Even where the interests of the business community are not at stake, video materials offer a special opportunity to exercise language talents and to increase cultural knowledge.

Perhaps the most obvious place for authentic international video materials is on television. I am thinking not about the programs scheduled on existing channels but about creative use of university television networks or local-access cable channels. Where copyright clearance can be obtained, local television systems provide a perfect arena for a regular foreign-language series or a distance-learning course. Such a series might include not only programs like those used in a classroom situation but also videos produced by a foreign class to exchange with a local class or video materials produced as part of an international sister-city program.

International video materials also belong in public library collections, as a welcome alternative to shelf upon shelf of feature films. Depending on the public served by the library, the cassettes selected might include travelogues with commentaries in the target language, fiction programs keyed to books available in the library, cassettes aimed at children, and even how-to programs such as lessons on cooking in French, pasta making in Italian, or cake decorating in German. In the future, programs of this type will surely become increasingly available.

As important as these general cultural applications of international video may be, I am convinced that they will be far outstripped by a growing business use of foreign-language video. Suppose your local bank has just decided to expand its international division. It may be unlikely that the local talent pool includes many people qualified to handle both the language and banking requirements of an internationally oriented position. Clearly some on-the-job training will be required. What better training is there for this kind of work than video programs depicting the various aspects of the financial world in Venezuela or Japan, with commentary in Spanish or Japanese? The many potential applications of this general logic suggest that international business concerns will in the near future avail themselves of this opportunity. Many businesses currently produce an annual report on video, while others train their personnel with videotapes or videodiscs. International video materials that target specific fields provide a double benefit. Not only do employees who use these materials develop their understanding of a particular aspect of the company's or a competitor's operations, they also absorb just the right vocabulary in the foreign language for dealing with that aspect of operations. Again, the necessary programs are not in every case currently available, but this is a market that cannot fail to grow significantly in the years to come.

Around the school, around the community, there are many places for foreign-language video. In grammar schools, international video programs have an important role to play in broadening children's experience. Learning about differences from the images while sensing differences in the language is an important experience for children of all ages. Video will, of course, play a special role in language immersion programs, in which children learn standard school subjects in a language that is not their first language. In the math part of a Francophone immersion school, a video program such as *Des chiffres et des lettres,* which makes a contest out of arithmetic operations, would be especially useful. Little by little, programs are appearing that make it increasingly worthwhile to envision a new kind of language education in the elementary schools, as well as an entirely new approach to teaching adults.

In the years to come, the increased availability of international programming is bound to change the way the community experiences its relationship to other cultures. Most Americans are interested only sporadically in foreign languages and cultures—after a trip abroad, while they play host to an exchange student, when a foreign film or play piques their curiosity. In the past, unfortunately, little reinforcement was available for that interest. The best that could be hoped for was perhaps a book to be ordered by the local book store with delivery in four to six weeks, an Alliance Française course starting in a month, or intermittent correspondence with the departed exchange student. In contrast, international video, whether borrowed from the local library, ordered by phone, or seen on cable TV, provides the kind of audiovisual reinforcement that stands a chance of sustaining the intermittent American interest in foreign languages and cultures.

Notes

1. See Chapter 10 for suggestions regarding equipment choice, operation, and maintenance.

2. Remember, though, that the copyright exemptions granted for face-to-face classroom use do not apply to scheduled language lab showings open to all students and not part of a specific course curriculum. If you are using off-air recordings or standard nontheatrical videocassettes, large public showings are probably not legal. See Chapter 9 for further information on legal concerns.

3. Not many tapes are now commercially available in these languages, or in dozens of other non-European languages, but in the coming years radical changes should occur on this front, as the negotiations currently undertaken by PICS and other organizations come to fruition.

4. The American tendency to concentrate language education on the early stages, stressing familiarity with the language for all rather than expertise for a few, has been the object of much recent commentary. The National Foreign Language Center in Washington, D.C., has made the expansion of advanced language education one of its basic concerns. See the center's inaugural position paper, signed by Richard Lambert.

PART III

Practical Considerations

CHAPTER 9

Video and the Law

How many angels can fit on the head of a pin? Citing seemingly senseless questions like this one, we often make fun of medieval theologians and their willingness to speculate on unresolvable problems. Who can say how many angels? How can we know for sure when we have the right answer? Surely God alone can provide the ultimate response, yet by the time we gain access to God's truth it will be too late to introduce it into human argument. In all too many ways, the subject of this chapter resembles a medieval debate. When is it legal to show a videotape? Who is qualified to judge? What will happen to those who make a wrong decision? Although the opinions stated in this chapter should not be taken as legal advice, they will at least help readers to understand the current complexity of video copyright problems. General familiarity with the principles involved should help teachers, media center directors, and administrators to make informed decisions.

Anyone who uses a videocassette recorder knows that the use of videotapes is subject to certain legal limitations. More and more purchased or rented cassettes have stickers advising, "This videocassette is for home use nonpublic exhibition in the United States of America and Canada only. Any other use is not authorized and is prohibited." The Motion Picture Association of America, Inc., has issued a warning similar to a no-trespassing sign:

Warning!

"For Home Use Only" Means Just That!

By law, as well as by intent, the prerecorded videocassettes and videodiscs available in stores throughout the United States are *for home use only.*

Sales of prerecorded video cassettes and videodiscs do not confer any public performance rights upon the purchaser.

The U.S. Copyright Act grants to the copyright owner the *exclusive* right, among others, "to perform the copyrighted work publicly." (United States Code, Title 17, Sections 101 and 106). Even "performances in 'semipublic' places such as clubs, lodges, factories, summer camps, and schools are 'public performances' subject to copyright control." (Senate Report No. 94-473, page 60; House Report No. 94-1476, page 64.)[1]

With warnings like this pasted onto prerecorded cassettes, it is hardly surprising that educators have doubts about their rights. Indeed, few people realize that educational use of videotapes undoubtedly constitutes the *most* complicated aspect of the video copyright problem.

Let us recognize from the start that we are not dealing with one problem here, but a series of related problems. Off-air copying presents different problems from using purchased prerecorded cassettes. The right to make and use multiple copies of a program is different from the right to show a single copy. Using videotapes in face-to-face teaching is not the same as broadcasting or cablecasting to remote locations. The legal status of satellite transmissions may depend on the country of origin. Perhaps more importantly, what is appropriate for a private citizen to do with video may be less appropriate for a teacher in the exercise of his or her duties and downright dangerous for an official responsible for the entire school's video needs. In spite of the complexity of the problem, however, certain principles seem clear.

Prerecorded Videocassettes

The United States Copyright Revision Act of 1976 was passed prior to the current video revolution. Consequently, it does not take fully into account certain current practices and expectations. Most common situations are, however, explicitly covered by the act. Section 106 reserves for the copyright holder the exclusive right to reproduce and sell the copyrighted work, as well as to perform or display it publicly. In the language of the act, to *perform* means to play the work; to *display* means to reproduce excerpted images. In general, then, the right to public performance can be granted only by the copyright holder.

Section 110, however, specifically excludes certain educational situations from the limitations prescribed by Section 106:

Notwithstanding the provisions of Section 106, the following are not infringements of copyright:
(1) performance or display of a work by instructors or pupils in the course of face-to-face teaching activities of a

nonprofit educational institution, in a classroom or similar place devoted to instruction, unless, in the case of a motion picture or other audiovisual work, the performance, or the display of individual images, is given by means of a copy that was not lawfully made under this title, and that the person responsible for the performance knew or had reason to believe was not lawfully made.[2]

In other words, educators in *nonprofit institutions* have the clear right to use *legally purchased* videocassettes in *face-to-face* teaching situations.

Although Section 110 of the Copyright Act grants clear rights in the most common teaching situations, other familiar uses of videotaped programs are not so distinctly defined. In particular, the Copyright Act places specific emphasis on the face-to-face nature of the exempted teaching activity. In addition, a report on the act by the House of Representatives insists that exempted performances be part of a systematic course of instruction and not provided for recreation or entertainment.[3] This is usually taken to mean that schools may not play home-use videotapes for assemblies or other out-of-class activities. More to the point for readers of this book, it probably means that language media centers may not organize public showings of foreign films or other home-use videotape programs, even if these showings are restricted to students (unless the programs involved explicitly allow such showings).

But may a language lab allow students, together or separately, to view a video program that is part of a particular course of instruction? In reality, it is an increasingly common practice for language labs to perform many of the tasks of language instruction, especially when electronic technology is involved. Even if language lab performance of instructional videotapes meets the *systematic course of instruction* test, however, it does not always satisfy the requirement that exempted performances take place in *face-to-face teaching situations*. In order to assure compliance with Section 110 of the Copyright Act, instructors would be well advised to make sure that all viewings intended to take place in the language lab be specifically mentioned in the course syllabus, thus guaranteeing that they are part of a systematic course of instruction. The instructor's presence at full-class viewings in the language lab or other location would provide further assurance that such viewings be considered face-to-face instructional performances. By the same token, language lab directors concerned to respect the letter of the law might well insist that all requests for course-related showings be accompanied by a syllabus that mentions the program to be shown.[4]

Although it grants special rights in face-to-face teaching situations, the Copyright Act of 1976 complicates matters for language lab directors, media programmers, and all others concerned with providing important educational video experiences outside the confines of specific courses.

There are three possible solutions for this important educational concern. Most obviously, one can contact the copyright holder in order to request public performance rights. More and more distributors and producers are prepared to grant public performance rights, usually for a price, but this solution does take time and effort, sometimes without satisfactory results. A more appropriate solution is to purchase tapes that already have the necessary educational clearances. Programs developed for an educational market are more likely to meet this requirement than feature films, but even educational programs cannot be assumed to carry public performance rights. A third alternative, which involves direct reception of foreign programs by cable or satellite, as well as off-air recording of these programs, is discussed more fully in the following section.

Off-Air Recordings

For many instructors, instant access to foreign-language programming has long represented an ideal, albeit seemingly unrealizable, solution. With the broadcast of international programs by satellite, the dreams of many have been realized. For many others, the educational promise of broadcast television has never been fulfilled. As discussed in Chapter 11, a drawback to broadcast television's immediacy lies in the difficulty, or even illegality, of capturing the broadcast signal for more carefully planned use at a later date. This section deals with the legality both of capturing domestic and international foreign-language broadcasts and of recording those broadcasts for future performances.

Theoretically, the legality of receiving and playing television broadcasts is quite complicated. The national laws of individual countries are complex and contradictory, as are the commercial practices of various networks and markets. Nevertheless, the practical aspects of simply receiving television signals may be reduced to one simple rule: as long as you are only receiving a television signal and neither recording the image nor charging a fee for viewing the image, then there is little chance that you will be considered to be violating the rights of the broadcasting station or of the program copyright holder. This is why language media centers with a satellite dish have felt justified in providing screenings of Russian- and French-language programming received from abroad, as well as Italian- and Spanish-language programs originating in this country.

Needless to say, just receiving the programs has limited educational benefits. Most of us want to be able to build appropriate programs into a systematic course of instruction. In order to do this, we need to be able to view many programs, choose the best ones, and then count on having the programs of our choice available for repeated use in class. As soon as we contemplate recording television programs, however, we enter a new jurisdiction, legally speaking. Insufficiently treated by the 1976 Copyright Act, the practice of off-air recording remained in limbo for many years, neither clearly permitted nor clearly proscribed. Since 1981, however, the situation of off-air recording has been for all practical purposes settled. Under the direction of Representative Robert W. Kastenmeier, a House subcommittee consulted interested parties from educational, producing, and broadcasting institutions. A set of practical guidelines that have since been widely, but not universally, recognized resulted from these consultations. Technically, these guidelines do not have the force of law. Practically, however, they define an appropriate set of practices, scrupulously adhered to by most language laboratories and media services. Here is the entirety of the House guidelines:

Guidelines for Off-Air Recording of Broadcast Programming for Educational Purposes

In March of 1979, Congressman Robert Kastenmeier, Chairman of the House Subcommittee on Courts, Civil Liberties and Administration of Justice, appointed a Negotiating Committee consisting of representatives of education organizations, copyright proprietors, and creative guilds and unions. The following guidelines reflect the Negotiating Committee's consensus as to the application of "fair use" to the recording, retention and use of television broadcast programs for educational purposes. They specify periods of retention and use of such off-air recordings in classrooms and similar places devoted to instruction and for homebound instruction. The purpose of establishing these guidelines is to provide standards for both owners and users of copyrighted television programs.

1. The guidelines were developed to apply only to off-air recording by non-profit educational institutions.

2. A broadcast program may be recorded off-air simultaneously with broadcast transmission (including simultaneous cable retransmission) and retained by a non-profit educational institution for a period not to exceed the first forty-five (45) consecutive calendar days after date of recording. Upon conclusion of such retention period, all off-air recordings must be erased or destroyed immediately. "Broadcast programs" are television programs transmitted by television stations for reception by the general public without charge.

3. Off-air recordings may be used once by individual teachers in the course of relevant teaching activities, and repeated

once only when instructional reinforcement is necessary, in classrooms and similar places devoted to instruction within a single building, cluster or campus, as well as in the homes of students receiving formalized home instruction, during the first ten (10) consecutive school days in the forty-five (45) day calendar day retention period. "School days" are school session days—not counting weekends, holidays, vacations, examination periods, or other scheduled interruptions—within the forty-five (45) calendar day retention period.

4. Off-air recordings may be made only at the request of and used by individual teachers, and may not be regularly recorded in anticipation of requests. No broadcast program may be recorded off-air more than once at the request of the same teacher, regardless of the number of times the program may be broadcast.

5. A limited number of copies may be reproduced from each off-air recording to meet the legitimate needs of teachers under these guidelines. Each such additional copy shall be subject to all provisions governing the original recording.

6. After the first ten (10) consecutive school days, off-air recordings may be used up to the end of the forty-five (45) calendar day retention period only for teacher evaluation purposes, i.e., to determine whether or not to include the broadcast program in the teaching curriculum, and may not be used in the recording institution for student exhibition or any other non-evaluation purpose without authorization.

7. Off-air recordings need not be used in their entirety, but the recorded programs may not be altered from their original content. Off-air recordings may not be physically or electronically combined or merged to constitute teaching anthologies or compilations.

8. All copies of off-air recordings must include the copyright notice on the broadcast program as recorded.

9. Educational institutions are expected to establish appropriate control procedures to maintain the integrity of these guidelines.[5]

Just what do these guidelines mean, and why have they been formulated in this particular way? In one sense, the guidelines provide an appropriate complement to the face-to-face teaching exemptions mentioned in the 1976 Copyright Act. Whereas the Copyright Act makes provision for educational use in the structured curriculum of a classroom situation but provides little leeway for general cultural and recreational use of video programs, the off-air recording guidelines make structured classroom use difficult, while creating the possibility of more general extracurricular use of off-air recorded programs. In an effort to satisfy educators' needs, while still protecting the important rights of copyright holders, legislators made it possible to extend the legal viewing period over ten school days, enough in legislators' opinion to permit scheduling of a special viewing of a topical program especially appropriate for a class currently underway.

According to these guidelines, after ten days educators can no longer use off-air recorded material in a classroom situation without infringing on the rights of the copyright holder. For another thirty-five days, however, teachers, but not students, may view the recorded programs to decide whether the school should attempt to acquire the rights necessary for using the programs in subsequent semesters. In theory, this appears to be a perfectly reasonable approach: free use for the short term, with long-term use predicated on acquisition of appropriate permission. In reality, however, it is well nigh impossible to obtain rights from an American network for educational use of broadcast programs, let alone a foreign network.[6] Indeed, given the state of laws governing the rights of actors, directors, and producers in some countries, some networks would rather not even be asked for releases.

Many individual instructors, and some schools, have decided to disregard the off-air recording guidelines on the grounds that they are impractical as regards foreign broadcasts and very difficult to enforce. Such a position is, I suggest, rather shortsighted. The following scenario may very likely occur. You keep a permanent copy of a particularly useful program, show it to interested colleagues and students one semester, then build it into a course the next. As time goes by, you spend untold hours developing related materials designed to make the program work better as part of a systematic course of instruction. The course goes well, so another section is opened and taught by a colleague from the materials you have prepared. With so many students, there is increasing pressure to deposit the tape at the language lab for drop-in viewing. At this point, you may have decided not to make any back-up copies, not wanting to stretch the law any further yet knowing full well that the sole copy may be erased at any moment. Alternatively, you have made the appropriate number of back-up copies for the size of the audience and the nature of your use. In that case, the felony has been compounded, and the likelihood of discovery and the seriousness of the offense have been maximized.

The impracticality of obtaining the necessary releases for permanent recording makes broadcast television a less-than-ideal basis for curriculum development. It makes sense to use off-air recordings only for the kind of topical enrichment that the original broadcasts provided and to find another source of programs that can legally be copied, retained, and shown in all appropriate educational situations.[7]

Making Copies

There are two contradictory realities to be resolved before copies may be made.

1. If you want to run a smooth, educationally viable program involving videotapes, then you must make as many copies as could possibly be needed, along with a file original as a back-up. Without the requisite number of copies, an instructor *is* in trouble. "Sorry, the tape is being used in class; come back next period." "Sorry, the new teacher took the tape home to prepare some vocabulary questions; come back tomorrow." "Sorry, the know-it-all in third period recorded over that program; come back when you find another copy . . ."

2. The more copies you make of a copyrighted program to which you do not have multiple-copy rights, the more liable you become if ever you or your institution is charged with copyright infringement. If all you have is your own copy of a foreign broadcast, the odds are that you will never be questioned. There is a strong precedent for using realia of all sorts in the teaching process. It is true that audiovisual texts are treated somewhat differently by the law, but it is difficult to imagine legal action being taken to preclude the educational use of single personal copies of realia, even when legal status is uncertain. If the requisite three copies for the sections of a Spanish conversation class are made, however, this argument becomes invalid. The only solution is to obtain the right to make multiple copies of all those programs that will be used on either a broad or a recurring basis.

How can one tell when the right to make copies is included in the price of a videocassette? An appropriate rule of thumb here is that any right not specifically accorded can be assumed to be reserved by the copyright holder. In other words, unless the catalogue or cassette specifies that copies may be made, you should assume that no copies may be legally made. In the case of prerecorded commercial cassettes, such as feature films, copies may almost never be made legally. As for off-air recordings, keeping even one copy more than forty-five days is illegal. Obviously, making further copies is also illegal.

With cassettes provided by educational or foreign-language distributors, however, it may be worthwhile to request permission to make a back-up master. Some companies will refuse, but others will recognize the unreasonableness of requiring students, or teachers, to use the only copy of a valuable program. Certain programs designate specific copying rights; for example, they may give the right to make an unlimited number of copies for educational use on a single campus. Other distributors will provide reduced-price copies to purchasers of a full-price original.

In the last analysis, you and your institution must make your own decisions regarding appropriate procedures. Before you decide to invest too much time integrating an illegal copy into your program, though, think ahead. Can you proudly display your work to a visitor from the Goethe Institute? Will you feel comfortable demonstrating your supplementary materials in support of a conference presentation? Will you hesitate to publish your materials in a prestigious professional journal, knowing that the program involved is not yet in the legal public domain? If any of these questions gives you pause, then you will probably feel uneasy, as the law says you should, about making multiple copies of the program and sharing it with a colleague at another institution. Now that video materials that may legally be copied are available, it would be a shame not to take advantage of them and profit from the open sharing that they foster.

Notes

1. Quoted in Jerome K. Miller, *Using Copyrighted Videocassettes in Classrooms and Libraries* (Champaign, Ill: Copyright Information Services, 1984), p. 57.

2. *United States Code,* Title 17, "Copyrights," Section 110.

3. U.S. House of Representatives, *Report No. 94-1476,* Section 106.

4. For further information and opinions regarding the use and copying of prerecorded video materials, see Miller, *Using Copyrighted Videocassettes in Classrooms and Libraries,* and Mary Hutchings Reed and Debra Stanek, "Library and Classroom Use of Copyrighted Videotapes and Computer Software," center insert in *American Libraries,* 17: No. 2 (1981), 5–13. Librarians should pay special attention to Miller's report of a controversy between Newton K. Minow and Burton H. Hanft over library use of prerecorded cassettes; see Miller, pp. 30–47, 59–63.

5. *Congressional Record,* October 14, 1981, E 4751.

6. Note, however, that some government-sponsored broadcasts may benefit from special extended retention periods specifically negotiated to

permit more fruitful educational usage. Each monthly installment of *France-TV Magazine,* the Antenne 2 program retransmitted by the University of Maryland–Baltimore County, for example, may be retained until May 31 of the academic year following the one in which it was first broadcast.

7. For further information and opinions on off-air recording, see R. D. Billings, "Off-the-Air Videorecording, Face-to-Face Teaching, and the 1976 Copyright Act," *Northern Kentucky Law Review,* 4 (1977), 225–51, and Esther R. Sinofsky, *Off-Air Videotaping in Education: Copyright Issues, Decisions, Implications* (New York: R. R. Bowker, 1984).

CHAPTER 10
Demystifying the Video Recorder

On some days, the videocassette recorder seems to me a heaven-sent solution to my teaching problems. On other days, it is the devil's instrument. If I go into a class with an unfamiliar VCR, I can be sure to lose control over the machine, lose my patience, and all too soon lose the students' attention as well. Even when all seems bleakest, however, there are a number of simple principles that can help me regain control over myself, the machine, and maybe even the students. Videocassette recorders are not complicated; but like other machines, they must be understood to be properly operated. Unfortunately, most operator's manuals concentrate so much on *which* button to push to get *which* effect that they never bother with the basic principles. Moreover, the operator's manual is an item rarely found with the VCR in most institutional situations. The present chapter provides the essential information that every instructor needs to know before venturing into a classroom in the company of a VCR.

Getting Started

A color television program is electronically encoded according to one of three basic *standards: SECAM* (used in France, the USSR, parts of Africa, and much of the Arab world), *PAL* (used in the rest of Europe, parts of Africa, parts of Asia, and the east coast of South America), and *NTSC* (used in North America, the west coast of South America, and most Far Eastern countries). If you use only American prerecorded tapes or off-air recordings made in the United States, then the question of standard need not concern you. If you plan to use videotapes sold or recorded abroad, however, be sure to obtain tapes recorded in NTSC. Otherwise, either access to a *multistandard* VCR or recourse to the expensive process of *standards conversion* (or *transcoding*) is needed.[1] (A multistandard VCR is recommended as a good investment for every language lab and library, since it increases significantly the number of foreign-language programs that can be played.)

Videocassettes exist in various *formats,* of which the most common are the 3/4″ *U-Matic* format and the two 1/2″ formats, *VHS* and *Beta,* the latter fast disappearing in favor of VHS. Since copies made from 1/2″ tapes tend to be of poor quality, by far the best solution is to use the 3/4″ U-Matic format for all masters, with all daily-use copies made on whichever 1/2″ format is recommended and serviced by your school's audiovisual technician or local video store.

A normal television set consists of two basic parts: a *tuner* that captures the incoming signal on any of the frequencies to which its channels are set, and a *monitor* that takes the signal and displays it as a continuous moving image. In many ways, a VCR is similar, for it conceals a tuner behind its more visible components. It is of course the existence of this separate tuner that makes it possible to record one program on a VCR while another is being viewed on the attached television set. In order to play a videocassette, we must arrange the settings of the attached television so that the signal reaching the screen comes not from the television's tuner but from the VCR. This task is facilitated by the fact that videocassette recorders routinely transmit signals on a frequency approximating that of U.S. channel 3 or 4. In order to display the image from your videotape, therefore, you must take the following steps:

1. Set the VCR to send the tape signal rather than the tuner signal to the television, normally by switching a button from TV to VIDEO, unless this is done automatically in your machine.

2. Set the television to select the signal coming from the VCR rather than the signal coming from the TV's own tuner by flipping a switch from TV to either VIDEO or VCR and by making sure that the television is set to channel 3 or 4 or some other channel setting that you and your technician have selected and regulated.

If you receive the expected image on your screen but find that it is somewhat deformed or partially obscured by unattractive bars, adjust the *tracking control* on your VCR. Normally, this is the only adjustment that should be needed.

If you are fortunate enough to have a VCR all to yourself, the preceding instructions may be unnecessary for you. For others, I cannot insist enough on the importance of attaching to both the VCR and the television or monitor complete instructions for the use of both. Even if everyone with access to the machine supposedly uses it for the same purposes and never changes the setting, the day may come when someone tunes in an important ball game and thus rearranges the set for TV reception just before your test on a video unit. Or perhaps someone will borrow a cable, hook up another machine, or even twist the dials.

If every VCR setup carries full instructions, like the ones reproduced here from the video lab at the University of Iowa, then putting things back in order will take a matter of minutes.

Instructions taped to the side of a Hitachi CMT 2060 multistandard monitor, which shares a cart with an AKAI VS-2EGN multistandard VTR (videotape recorder).

Instructions for Use of the Machines on This Cart

1. Plug in the extension cord wound around one end of cart.
2. Turn on the power switch (attached to power strip on one side of cart).
3. Turn on television and videotape recorder.
4. Push EJECT to expose the tape insertion mechanism.
5. Insert tape (push down entire mechanism gently to engage).
6. Open panel below TV trade name and make sure that TV/VTR button on right is pushed in (set for VTR) and that PAL-SECAM/NTSC button next to it designates proper standard (out for NTSC, i.e. normal American-standard tapes).
7. Push PLAY. Image should appear.

If the image appears but has bars or other interference, adjust the tracking control located under the left front of the VTR. If after a few seconds the image fails to appear, make sure that the cart is plugged into a live outlet, that both TV and VTR are plugged into the cart's power strip, and that the power strip, TV, and VTR are turned on. Then check the rear panel of the VTR.

—Is the power cord plugged in (lower left-hand corner)?
—Is the rear power switch on (upper left-hand corner)?
—Are the video out and audio out cords attached to the appropriate TV inputs (VTR video out to TV video in, VTR audio out to TV audio in)?

If the image still does not appear, check your cassette; you may be in a section with no programming. Try rewinding to the beginning and starting the process over again. If all is to no avail, contact the Language Media Center for further instructions (125 Schaeffer Hall, telephone 335-2331; open from 8 A.M.–8 P.M. Monday through Friday and from 9 A.M.– 1 P.M. Saturday).

When you have finished, remove your tape by pressing EJECT, close the tape insertion mechanism, turn off the TV, VTR (front upper left only—don't touch the rear power switch), and power strip. Unplug the cart, rewind the extension cord as you found it, and return the cart to 106 Schaeffer Hall. If you have checked out a remote control unit, don't forget to have it checked back in; otherwise you will be charged for it.

Classroom Use

Videocassette recorders work very much like familiar audiocassette recorders. In order to record or play, the audio recorder brings the sound heads into contact with the tape, which a motor drives at a constant, slow speed. The same motor is capable of advancing or rewinding the tape at a much faster speed, as long as the heads are not in contact with the tape. The main difference between the two machines lies in the fact that the VCR takes the tape to the heads rather than just bringing the heads to the tape. Seemingly minor, this difference is in fact of enormous importance for smooth classroom operation.

Let us call the two VCR modes of operation the *play* mode and the *rewind* mode. In the rewind mode, the machine simply inserts a motor-driven axle into each hole of the cassette. Without removing the tape from the cassette, the machine then advances or rewinds the tape at high speed, according to the function chosen (fast forward or rewind). The actual location of the tape in the rewind mode looks something like the following diagram:

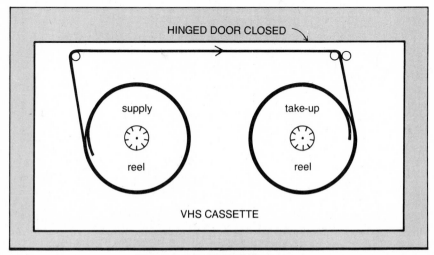

Tape path in REWIND mode
(Stop, Rewind, Fast Forward)

While the machine is in the rewind mode, no image appears on the screen, since the tape is not engaged on the playing heads.

In order for an image to appear on the screen, the tape must be drawn slowly and carefully out of the cassette and ingested into a prearranged configuration that brings it into contact with the playing heads, which move into position after the tape is in place. Different videocassette recorders handle the play mode in different ways, but the result usually looks something like the following:

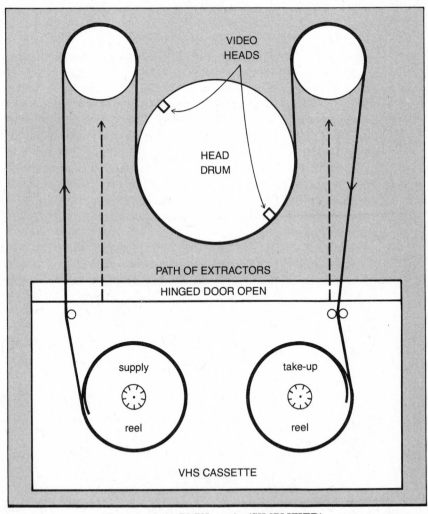

Tape path in PLAY mode (SIMPLIFIED)
(Play, Pause, Record, Visible Forward and Reverse)

The play mode is used not only for normal play but also for record, still-frame, and visible advance/reverse functions, known also by various trade names specific to individual brands. When there is an image on the screen or when the VCR is being held in readiness to produce an image instantaneously, the tape is in the play mode. The important point to note here is that it takes time for the machine to change modes, unless it has a *quick start* system that keeps the tape continually in the play mode.

If you are playing a tape and you want to see part of a scene again, you have two choices. One choice is to press the rewind button. (On some machines it is necessary to press the stop button first.) The heads recede, and the tape returns to its storage position in the cassette. Only then does the high-speed rewind motor turn on. When you reach the part of the scene to be reviewed and press the play button, the process is reversed: the tape is pulled out of the cassette and ingested by the machine, the heads move into place, and the slow-speed play motor is engaged. The entire process takes no more than half a minute, but anyone who has used this method in front of a class knows just how long those thirty seconds can seem.

If, on the other hand, you choose the visible reverse (search) function, the play motor simply stops, reverses direction, and starts up at a higher speed. Instead of a black screen, guaranteed to disperse student attention, the image stays on the screen—running backwards, of course. As soon as you release the visible reverse button (or, on some machines, hit the play button again), the motor reverses again and automatically kicks into the correct speed for normal playing. All this takes just a few seconds, with no delay, no dark screen, no dead time, no dulled attention.

The ability to remain in the play mode without damaging the machine is characteristic of almost all current VCRs. Whereas many earlier recorders had to be fully stopped and returned to the rewind mode between all commands, current machines permit direct movement between functions, with a consequent gain of time and convenience for those who understand the basic principles involved. Fast forward and reverse are generally capable of moving the tape many times faster than visible forward or reverse, so they are necessary for rewinding entire tapes or moving to the final scene of a feature film. However, as long as in-class VCR use can be designed around relatively short sequences, the ability to keep the tape in the play mode—whether through play, visible forward and reverse, or pause—will save precious seconds and conserve hard-won student interest.

Learning to use video in the classroom is not unlike learning ventriloquism. Rule 1 states that as long as the "dummy" is visible, it should remain active. Rule 2 suggests that the less interesting the "dummy's" activities, the more you have to work at keeping the audience's attention. In particular, if you have to fast-forward the tape to another sequence, do not stand next to the screen while the VCR whirrs away. If possible, move to the other side of the room and ask a question, so that students are not tempted to pay attention to the educationally sterile blank screen.

Keeping student attention focused on yourself and thus on organized teaching activity is much easier if you have a wireless remote control that governs all the major functions necessary for classroom activity. These functions are play, pause and stop, visible forward and reverse, fast forward and reverse, and even sound level, frame search, and contrast or brightness on some newer models. The more you can learn to work your video without seeming to pay attention to it, the more effective the video will be. From this comes rule 3: know your video. You would not enter a Grand Prix race in a car you had never driven; do not enter a classroom with a tape you have not seen or a VCR you have not practiced driving.

Choosing Equipment

What videocassette recorder or recorders you choose will certainly depend on a variety of concerns that cannot be discussed here, such as size of school, number of units that share machines, budget, special applications, and availability of local service, as well as new technological developments and other unforeseen changes. Nevertheless, basic information about the options available is necessary for everyone involved in the decision-making process. The most important decisions, in nearly every case, relate to 1/2″ machines: how many to buy, what features to look for, and so forth. The following list covers the major features offered today, roughly in order of importance to language teachers.

Essential Features

Play, Stop, Fast Forward and Reverse, Multiple-speed Playback. No single-standard machine on the market today fails to offer these basic functions. Multiple-speed playback, which permits the playing of tapes recorded in the extended-play mode, is available on very few multistandard machines.

Visible Forward and Reverse. These are absolutely essential functions. If possible, choose a machine that does not require the button to be held down in order for these functions to continue.

Pause. For a foreign language instructor, this is a must, even if only to keep the tape from going merrily on its way while you are trying to explain a difficult cultural reference. The clearer the frozen image, the more likely you will be able to do careful in-class—or, for that matter, at-home—image analysis. If a clear still image is especially important to you, choose a VCR with four video heads, an arrangement that provides more stable still images. Be sure that the machine automatically returns to play after a limited time in pause, because remaining in pause too long can permanently damage the tape.

Remote Control. This is essential for use in a large classroom. If you do acquire machines with wireless remote control, be sure to establish an ironclad check-out policy for the remote control units. Some remote control units govern only a few functions, so be sure to check that your units control visible forward, visible reverse, and pause, as well as the less useful channel selection and fast forward and reverse functions.

Desirable Features for at Least One Machine

Record. Every lab certainly needs at least one machine that records. However, putting recorders in the hands of teachers and students will actually only increase the potential for trouble. The cheaper machines do not come in player-only versions, and the player-only versions of the better machines are often in the same price range as the fully equipped models of lighter-duty VCRs. One feature that you will not be able to avoid, but that you should not use, is the capacity to record at multiple speeds. As with sound recording, only the fastest speed will produce fidelity appropriate for the teaching of a foreign language.

Programmable Recording. Unless you already have some arrangement for off-air recording, you should have at least one VCR with an easy-to-use and versatile automatic recording function. As more and more foreign programs become available by satellite, often during the night, programmable recording will certainly become increasingly important.

Second Sound Track. All 3/4″ recorders have this feature, but only the commercial-quality 1/2″ machines can read two sound tracks separately. Although not all your machines need this feature, you will want at least one that can take advantage of programs for which a simplified second sound track has been prepared. Otherwise, you will have to buy two copies of the program in order to get both sound tracks.

Audio Dub. This feature permits you to record a new sound track without disturbing the original picture.

Frame Search or Automatic Zeroing. These extremely useful features permit you to go to a specific time or counter number. You either simply dial that number, punch a button on the most sophisticated models, or press rewind and the tape will stop at the point where the counter was last set at zero, that is, at the beginning of the sequence to be used in class. An even more useful recent variation, called *indexing*, involves insertion of electronic index markers at desired points—for example, at the beginnings of scenes to be studied in class. The machine can perform an automatic search of each index. (See photo, p. 81.)

Headphone Jack. Although headphone jacks are not needed for classroom units, they are desirable for setups that may be used in a language lab, unless the monitor already has a jack.

Optional Functions

Slow Motion, Frame-by-frame Advance, Fancy Features. I have found that variable-speed slow motion and other features "guaranteed to impress your friends" do not actually get used much in language classes. However, they do crowd the instrument cluster with infrequently used buttons and add just one more item to go wrong. This statement assumes that your machines are used only for language instruction; if they also serve for film analysis, additional features may be extremely desirable.

Many other options are available, of course, from the relatively common shuttle search (a single knob that controls visible advance and reverse, as well as tape speed) to the various professional editing functions. If you need and can afford any of this sophistication, by all means proceed, but remember that only a few trained individuals will use these sophisticated functions. Make sure that the more modest needs of students and teachers are met by a sufficient number of more modest machines.

The choice of televisions or monitors is much easier. Do not choose a behemoth; anything over 23″ can be hard to move around. In addition, do not spend money on fancy options; remote control, for example, is needed for the VCR, not the television. Concentrate instead on overall quality, a good image, and above all good sound, which is hard to find on all but specialized models. Remember that a multistandard VCR will require a multistandard monitor.[2]

Just as important as the VCR and monitor, but rarely given serious consideration, is the cart used to transport them from one room to another. Unless all your classrooms are equipped with video equipment, you will want to make sure that sufficient mobile units are available for each building in which language classes are taught. Locked up while not in use, these units can easily be moved from room to room as long as sufficient thought and money has gone into the purchase of appropriate carts. The carts should be sturdy, roll easily—that is, have wheels big enough not to be stopped by cracks, thresholds, and the like—and not be top-heavy. Try fully loading a cart before choosing. Personally, I do not care for the five-foot-high carts typically provided by audiovisual services at conferences around the country. They may be suitable for crowded conference rooms, but they are top-heavy, hard to control, and not generally appropriate for language classes. Far better is the desk-high model, with VCR at knee height. It can double as a work station in the lab, whereas the larger carts just sit around and take up room. An incorporated outlet strip is a godsend, especially if it includes an easily stored cord long enough to reach the most inconveniently located wall outlet.

The equipment world does not stop with the standard VCR/monitor/cart unit, but it would take too much space to range across videodisc players, video/computer interfaces, projection televisions, and the like. Two pieces of advice must suffice for now. First, leave room on your video carts for a videodisc player, which will certainly grow in usefulness and popularity with the increasing selection of programs available on videodisc. Second, if possible, always consult someone who already owns the equipment you are thinking of buying.

Language Lab Procedures and Arrangements

Anyone who runs a successful language laboratory knows that a few lines or even a few pages are insufficient to suggest all the procedures involved in this task. This section thus provides no blueprint for the successful operation of a video facility but only a few tips for those with limited experience in this area.

The Care and Feeding of Machines

Once your units have been set up, anchor each machine to its cart whenever possible, either by fastening it on with a cable security device or by replacing the screw that holds the feet on with a similar screw driven through the cart shelf from the bottom. This will increase stability and reduce the incidence of VCR disappearance. For units that are meant to be wheeled to class, mounting a sign-up sheet right on the cart will help avert faculty squabbles. Make sure that all units are checked systematically on a regular basis for mechanical problems such as frayed cables, faulty connections, and poor image quality. Sometimes a simple setting can make all the difference.

Tape Maintenance

If possible, keep 3/4″ masters of all tapes in a safe place. That way no one will be tempted to borrow the master for in-class use. You can guard against recording over an important program by breaking off a small plastic tab on each cassette. Assuming that appropriate copyright clearance has been obtained, 1/2″ copies can be made for faculty and student use. Connections on 3/4″ machines require plugs different from those on 1/2″ machines, so do not assume that the cables that came with either machine can be used interchangeably. The accompanying diagram illustrates the most common arrangement for copying a 3/4″ master onto a 1/2″ tape.

Be sure to establish a complete and standardized labeling process, including name of program, master number, standard (if you have multistandard equipment), date the copy was made, date it must be erased according to fair-use guidelines, and some indication, such as a letter or an asterisk, that there is further information on the tape in a file kept in the lab. This paper file should keep materials such as background information, transcript, exercises, and so on. Videotapes must be stored vertically to keep the tape from curling, in their dust jackets, and preferably in an environment in which heat and humidity are controlled. The checkout system should be foolproof or, sooner or later, language lab personnel and faculty may come to blows.

If you have appropriate copyright clearance, you may also want to make audio copies of videotapes, thus permitting students to play their video homework on small audio recorders. These copies also should be referenced in your paper file.

Arranging Language Lab Space

To say that most language labs are not configured for video usage is an understatement: most do not even have room for video carts, let alone space for viewing. This is no minor problem. The solutions suggested here are of two kinds: make-do solutions for institutions without a lab or for labs without room for video and more elaborate plans for permanent installations.

For the time being, many of you, especially in high schools and small colleges, will have to put up with a video unit wandering from classroom to classroom. Under these circumstances, by all means invest in a box that permits multiple headphones to be used simultaneously. Make sure that your cart is of the desk-height type, so that it can be used by individuals as well as whole classes. Try to create a video corner for permanent storage of video-related realia—things like foreign television

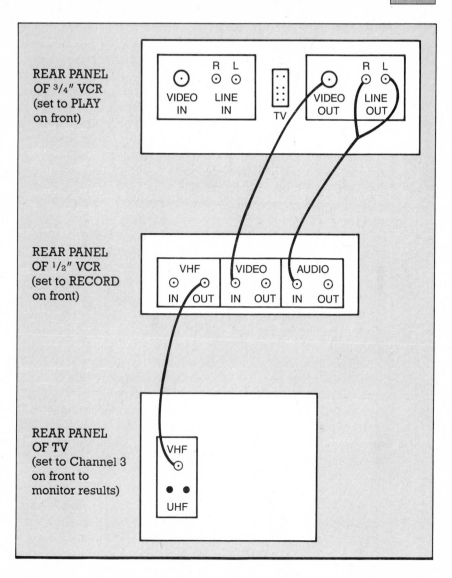

BASIC HOOKUP FOR MAKING A ¹/₂″ COPY FROM A ³/₄″ MASTER:
(Note that ³/₄″ plugs are usually bigger than ¹/₂″ plugs, necessitating a
special cable or reducer. Be sure to listen to both audio channels
separately on the ³/₄″ tape in order to decide whether you need to record
one channel alone or both channels together.)

programming guides, information on programs in current use, and so forth. In a high school, it may be a good idea to have the library handle tape storage and check-out, so that everyone will always know where to find a record of a tape's whereabouts. In fact, a library is a good place to locate a shared video unit equipped with headphones.

If you have been able to wangle a classroom for use as a video lab, make sure that it is permanently supervised and that cassettes are never actually left in the open. Try to avoid setting up video units in a nice neat row like audio booths. Although there are certainly times when individual students will have reason to work independently with separate programs, our experience at the University of Iowa suggests that viewing is often best done in small groups. Students can be assigned small-group activities that encourage them to interact during the viewing or to alternate viewing and speaking. Even without prescribed activities, students tend to want to talk to each other about the program, exchanging opinions and information in English at first but eventually in the target language. The addition of even a few room dividers makes it possible to arrange a classroom into a video lab that will accommodate group viewing. When the principal or dean approves the outfitting of a new lab, plan a number of small rooms appropriate for group video viewing by from four to six students.

The accompanying diagrams suggest two ways of organizing a lab to take advantage of video-engendered interaction. The first arrangement shows a temporary video lab installed in a classroom. Capable of being used in virtually any empty space, this partitioned arrangement provides maximum separation (and thus an opportunity for private conversation among students) and maximum space use. Complete classes as well as individuals can use the same space with a minimum rearrangement of partitions.[3]

The second diagram, which shows plans for the University of Iowa's proposed Language Media Center, suggests a possible model for new construction. Note that the small viewing cubicles along one side are large enough to accommodate six students and can double as conference rooms, recording booths, cart storage areas, teacher preview booths, and so forth. Single viewing booths equipped with headphones are located in the central carrel area.

Many of the technologies now thought of as applicable solely to individualized instruction (computer-assisted instruction, computer-controlled videotape, and videodisc) are in fact extremely productive when designed for and used in small-group situations. The viewing booths set aside for video viewing may also eventually double as spaces for computer-controlled videodisc work, as well as for the dubbing of second sound tracks and other recording or editing activities.

We are just beginning to understand how to create environments that make the best educational use of video technology and equipment.

Temporary Video Lab
$^3/_{16}'' = 1$ foot

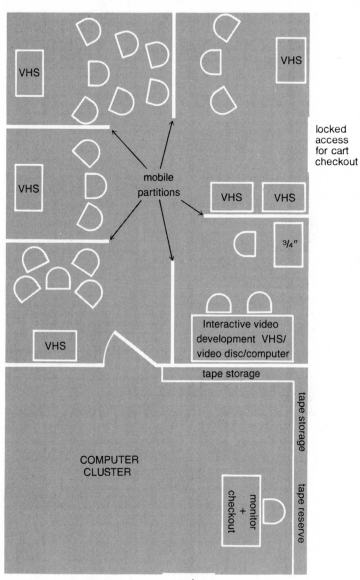

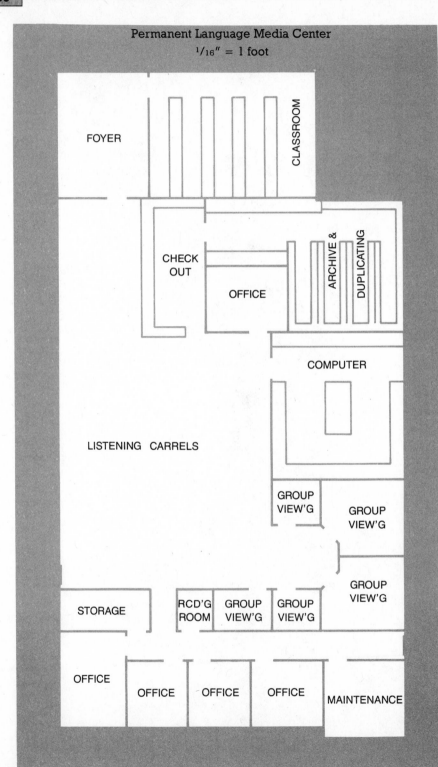

Permanent Language Media Center
$^1/_{16}'' = 1$ foot

This chapter has provided no more than a few suggestions derived from the experience of those who have been living with the problem for a few years.

Notes

1. For further information on standards and modes, as well as information on multistandard equipment and suggestions on how to handle tapes acquired abroad, see Rick Altman, "Access to International Television," *Studies in Language Learning,* 5: no. 1 (1985), 17–24.

2. See footnote 1.

3. At the University of Iowa this "video cluster" is entered through a "computer cluster" and thus benefits from the presence of the person monitoring the computer cluster. Some supervision of a video cluster is, of course, needed, not only for purposes of security but also to provide necessary tapes and technical assistance. The simplest way to provide this supervision is to arrange the video cluster so it can be entered only through the existing lab. An alternate arrangement is to place the video lab next to the library so that it can be supervised by library staff.

CHAPTER 11
Sources of Video Programming

It may seem strange that a book on foreign-language video should *end* with a chapter on sources of foreign-language video programming. After all, isn't the program the starting point for all video-based teaching? This has been the assumption of most educators who, over the years, have encouraged the use of video materials in the education process. In the past, the typical video unit began with a video program wedged into an apparently appropriate course at a propitious point. This pattern was not surprising in a world where foreign video materials were few and far between. With the advent of new channels of access to foreign video programming, we are now able to choose our programs more carefully. Just as the initial decision to use video is based on an integrated approach to the learning process, so the choice of video materials may now be seen as logically dependent on educational strategies, rather than the reverse.

The current chapter is divided into two parts. The first half analyzes the educational and practical benefits and drawbacks of the four major programming sources: foreign programs recorded abroad, foreign programs recorded off-air in this country (usually through satellite reception), international foreign-language video programs available for purchase in the United States, and American-produced foreign-language programs. The second part of the chapter provides an annotated list of sources for foreign-language programming in the United States, including commercial distributors, national cultural services, and other outlets.

Benefits and Drawbacks of Major Sources

Foreign Programs Recorded Abroad

Language teachers abroad are like children in toy stores. So excited are we to find plentiful examples of authentic language and culture that we want to bring it all home. Television programs are common targets for this international acquisitiveness. Sit and watch another country's television programming for a few hours and you are bound to want to bring it home alive. A decade ago, this was an impossible dream; today it does not take too much effort to find a friend with a videocassette recorder. Pen pals used to wield pens and send letters; now they have turned to the videocassette recorder, with tapings from local TV typically complementing homemade video. We *can* acquire foreign programs recorded abroad; but do we always *want* to?

Programs recorded abroad have two major drawbacks. First, with the exception of certain countries on the Pacific rim, the rest of the world uses a color broadcasting standard different from the American standard. This means that all tapes from Europe, Africa, and Australia, as well as most of those from Asia and South America, cannot be played on American televisions. To be sure, these tapes come in familiar VHS and Beta formats, but you can as easily receive FM broadcasts on your AM radio as play PAL or SECAM programs on standard NTSC equipment. The tape is exactly the same, but it plays at a different speed, has its information encoded in a different manner, carries its sound track differently, and calls for display of a larger number of lines. This is true whether the tape is a commercial prerecorded tape, an off-air copy, or even a copy made by a friend with a multistandard videocassette recorder. The latter does not *convert* the tape but only permits its display in the original standard on an appropriate television or monitor. Therefore, if you do not already own multistandard equipment or have inexpensive access to the normally expensive standards conversion process, then do not buy videotapes in a non-NTSC country.

The second problem is that of legal status. Although many countries recognize individuals' rights to make and keep a personal-use copy of a television broadcast, the performance of such videotapes in a public place is universally disallowed. Continued classroom use of off-air copies is thus not legal. Purchased copies, however, may have a different status. Although most countries offer little for sale beyond feature films, the commercial market should not be neglected as a potentially important source, assuming, of course, that your equipment can handle non-NTSC tapes. Look as well for educational distributors. You will not find these advertised in the mass media, but you may find them listed in the yellow pages of a large city's phone directory. Perhaps a colleague at a cooperating institution abroad can help you locate alternate sources.

For most people, technical difficulties and limited access reduce the feasibility of using programs recorded abroad. Such programs are nevertheless particularly useful for cinema courses, where simultaneous access to multistandard equipment and foreign video catalogues can radically change the corpus of films to which students are exposed. The same is true for civilization courses when archival footage or other historical materials are available for sale.

Foreign Programs Recorded in the United States

With the growth of satellite relays in the eighties, international broadcasting has become an imminent possibility, if not a current actuality. Today a few foreign-language programs are carried on national networks, such as Latin American programming on the Spanish International Network (SIN) and original-version foreign-language films on Bravo, Cinemax, and other pay channels. In addition, many metropolitan areas have some local-interest foreign-language programming—for example, Italian-language programs from the Italian Television Network (RAI) in numerous areas, French-language programs from Antenne 2 in New York and Louisiana, and Russian-language programs in scattered locations. Some foreign-language programming is broadcast by university-based projects; examples include the monthly Antenne 2 French news digest sponsored by the University of Maryland–Baltimore County and the more global efforts of Father Lee Lubbers and his pioneering SCOLA organization at Creighton University. In short, far more programs are now or will soon be available to those who can intercept satellite-relayed broadcasts originally destined for the home market. Thus Soviet television programs can be watched by those who can track and receive signals from the nongeostationary satellite Molniya. New Englanders with the right equipment can receive European programming by satellite. All across the northern portion of the United States, Canadian transmissions relayed by satellite can be received. As we move into the nineties, the number of foreign-language broadcasts that can be received by satellite can be expected to grow by leaps and bounds.

In assessing how relevant such programs are to the teaching of language and culture, we should consider separately two different potential uses. As a source of cultural enrichment, these broadcasts are unsurpassed. Even without understanding Russian, Americans can gain a great deal of understanding from watching Russian television. Perception about the Soviet peoples is sharpened by exposure to Russian aerobics or motorcycle polo, played with an oversized ball and a lot of guts. If your institution has access to satellite reception, by all means try to arrange a regular viewing of live television. If possible, maintain a balance between (a) absolutely live reception, which offers no chance of selecting the program but which preserves a sense of intensity and timeliness, and (b) carefully chosen recorded programs, which may be held for later viewing for up to ten school days. In order to know what programs will appear on what satellite at what time, you might subscribe to one of the growing number of satellite-oriented magazines.

For classroom use, these broadcast programs have somewhat less appeal. Even when the instructor knows exactly what time a program will appear, there is no guarantee that a class will be able to be present to watch the program. The instructor can record the program and use the recording in class, but he or she will not know what is in the program until it has appeared, and that may be too late to accommodate a change in the syllabus. Even if the program is just right, the instructor will have to prepare materials on short notice in order to get the greatest educational value out of the program. Then, once the instructor has spent time preparing supporting materials, the troubling question remains of whether the tape will be kept illegally for use in a later semester. All in all, this process is so unpredictable and time-consuming that it is probably best reserved for those few courses that legitimately depend on day-to-day social problems for their basic topic of discussion: current affairs, conversation courses concentrating on controversial subjects, civilization courses that stress understanding of contemporary problems, and the like.

International Foreign-language Video Materials Available for Purchase in the United States

Until recently, the only authentic foreign video programs available for purchase in the United States were feature films. Videotapes of feature films may not be easy to show to large groups, but they clearly have numerous advantages over 16mm copies for use with the average class. They are less expensive, are smaller and lighter, are generally in better overall condition, have higher-quality sound tracks, and are easier to preview at home. In addition, video copies are much easier to use in class, since they require no projection booth, screen, or projectionist. A single scene can be much more easily located, replayed, or presented with only sound or only image. Nevertheless, as noted in Chapter 2, feature films have serious drawbacks as teaching aids for all but the most advanced students.

Numerous organizations, recognizing both the benefits of video and the need for another type of program beyond feature films, have begun during the past few years to distribute international foreign-language video programs. These programs are produced for broadcast television by foreign countries or independent studios, for educational purposes by government-sponsored producers or commercial enterprises, and for public relations use by private companies or public entities such as the European Economic Community and the French Post Office. Not only do these programs have all the advantages of video distribution, but they are commonly distributed on American-standard cassettes and generally carry full clearance for educational use of all types. As long as they are available at a reasonable price, international foreign-language video materials available for purchase in the United States constitute the perfect teaching medium. Devoid of the technical problems of 16mm film, the standards problems of cassettes recorded abroad, and the copyright problems of off-air recordings, these programs deserve to be used in virtually all educational situations and can easily be purchased by colleagues at other institutions who may be anxious to share supporting materials.

Moreover, many distributors provide transcripts, workbooks, and teaching suggestions along with the basic cassette. Houghton Mifflin Company provides a teacher's guide or a workbook with its Spanish programs and a teacher's guide with its German programs. D. C. Heath now publishes a workbook to accompany a tape of ninety-seven French commercials originally published by Hachette in France. Each of the three tapes in the *La Télé des Français* series, jointly produced by Middlebury College and the Université de Paris IX-Dauphine, comes with a packet of materials giving suggestions for classroom use. The Project for International Communication Studies (PICS) provides a variety of supporting materials to accompany many of its cassettes. Numerous programs are

Sécurité routière is a series of short films appropriate for beginning language learners of all ages. Each 10-minute film first shows, without commentary, the dangerous habits and bothersome pranks of children, then reveals the way they should have acted. Here, the brother keeps his sister from darting in front of a Paris bus.

provided with a complete or partial transcript or a summary of contents. Others are accompanied by extensive suggestions for ways to integrate particular programs into specific courses, as well as samples of appropriate exercises. Still others are matched by specially designed workbooks developed by PICS personnel and distributed by a traditional publisher.

The range of international foreign-language video programs available for purchase is growing every year. The scope of materials includes news programs from nearly a dozen countries, theatrical performances and literary adaptations, broadcast television programs of various types, advertisements, educational programs, public relations programs, and many others. Still in short supply are international video materials specifically aimed at K-12 language programs and specially prepared tapes appropriate for use in the first year of language study. In the years to come, it seems likely that an increasing range of international programs in the American standard will become available with copyright clearance and even, in certain cases, with the right to make multiple copies for use on the purchasing campus.

American-produced Foreign-Language Video Materials

With the increasing demand for video programs keyed to American needs, American media-oriented foundations and publishers have begun to invest significant amounts of money and energy in producing foreign-language video materials for the American market. By and large, these programs display the expected strengths and weaknesses. Since they are created for a specific situation, they are better suited for use in that situation than the average program borrowed from a foreign television network. Conversely, since they are self-consciously created for American use, these American-made programs often sacrifice authenticity for clarity and a perfect match with a particular textbook or method. No global judgment can be made on these programs, for they vary widely in both conception and realization.

Currently available American foreign-language videocassettes fall into three basic categories. First are the programs supervised by a language teacher and made with a modest budget; willing, picturesque subjects; and a lively scenario. Bernard Petit has made fine examples of this type of video for Heinle & Heinle, and CALICO is distributing an interesting program, *VELVET,* produced in Germany with a combination of native speakers and actors in unrehearsed authentic situations. The second category includes animations, cartoons, and films using authentic stories and visual materials from the target culture, such as the Grimm and Perrault versions of *Little Red Riding Hood* made by PICS using contemporary German drawings and nineteenth-century French folk images from Epinal, recreated and colored by computer graphic means. Finally, we have recently seen a return to the complete telecourse with *French in Action* by Pierre

Using familiar tales assures comprehension even at the lowest levels and with students of all ages. Shown is a scene from Perrault's "Little Red Riding Hood" and the arrival of the woodsman in Grimm's version of the same tale. (*Little Red Riding Hood*)

Capretz of Yale University and Barry Lydgate of Wellesley College, with funds provided by the Annenberg/Corporation for Public Broadcasting Project and technical know-how contributed by WGBH of Boston. Foreign-language video materials shot in this country with backgrounds improvised so as not to look too American and actors chosen for their native accents and "authentic" features could form a fourth category. No doubt these programs have their usefulness, but too much authenticity is lost in simulating foreign locations to justify major use of such programs.

Of course, choice of materials depends heavily on personal preference, though readers of this book may want to consult the suggestions regarding choice of materials made in Chapters 2 and 3. The following list of sources should provide an appropriately broad selection. In general, this list concentrates on sources of international foreign-language video materials available for purchase in the United States. While some specialized distributors of feature films have been included, emphasis is on other types of programming. Each entry includes the distributor's name, address, and phone number, along with the variety and number of foreign-language programs available and the price range. In some cases a few comments on materials or service have been added.

Distributors of International Video Materials

Purchase prices quoted are for VHS videocassettes; Beta videocassettes are sometimes slightly higher; U-Matic videocassettes are always somewhat higher. Prices are subject to change.

Agency for Instructional Technology (Box A, Bloomington, Ind. 47402-0120; tel. 812/339-2203 or 800/457-4509). Primarily a developer of video materials for public schools. Distributors of the 1970 French Ministry of Foreign Affairs program, *En français* (twenty-six 15-minute programs, $125 per program).

Annenberg/Corporation for Public Broadcasting Project (1111 16th Street NW, Washington, D.C. 20036; tel. 800/LEARNER or 202/955-5251). The Annenberg/CPB project is the major sponsor of *French in Action,* the complete telecourse conceived and produced by Pierre Capretz of Yale University in collaboration with Barry Lydgate of Wellesley College and WGBH of Boston. The videocassette portion of the course includes twenty-six 60-minute cassettes ($650 for the entire set, $29.95 for individual cassettes). Print and audio materials are available through Yale University Press, 92A Yale Station, New Haven, Conn. 06520.

Asia Society, Education Department (725 Park Avenue, New York, N.Y. 10021; tel. 212/288-6400). Distributes programs entitled *Letters,* aimed at promoting understanding of Japanese culture ($17.50 per cassette).

CALICO (3078 JKHB, Brigham Young University, Provo, Utah 84601; tel. 801/378-7079). Distributors of *VELVET,* a program recorded in Germany (two-sided, double-sound-track videodisc, $195; single-sound-track VHS cassette, $95; audio cassettes and transcript also available).

CBS Fox Video (39000 7 Mile Rd., Livonia, Mich. 48152; tel. 313/591-1555). Distributors of the Rassias method videocassettes: *Contact French* (ten lessons, 45–75 minutes each, $995) and *Accent French* (43 minutes, $200).

College Film Center (322 South Michigan Ave., Chicago, Ill. 60604-4382; tel. 312/922-6621). Rental distributors for the International Film Bureau, Inc. (See entry for International Film Bureau, Inc.)

D. C. Heath and Company (125 Spring Street, Lexington, Mass. 02173; tel. 617/860-1530 or 800/235-3565). Distributes *97 publicités télévisées,* originally developed by Hachette (60 minutes, $250 for nonadopters of Heath textbooks, sliding price scale for adopters), along with an accompanying workbook written by Gerald Honigsblum. Videotape orders should be addressed to the Heath Distribution Center, 2700 N. Richardt Avenue, Indianapolis, Ind. 46219.

Democracy in Communication: Popular Video and Film in Latin America (124 Washington Place, New York, N.Y. 10014; tel. 212/463-0108). Distributes selected broadcast television materials from Mexico, Brazil, Chile, Peru, Panama, Bolivia, Uruguay, El Salvador, and Nicaragua (eight 60-minute tapes, $500 per set for purchase, $300 per set for rental; prices for individual tapes based on ability to pay).

EMC Publishing (300 York Avenue, Saint Paul, Minn. 55101; tel. 612/771-1555 or 800/328-1452). Distributes Wolfgang Kraft's *Deutsch: Aktuell,* which is accompanied by videocassettes made up of the sound and filmstrip material ($248 for five videocassettes).

Facets Multimedia Center (1517 West Fullerton Avenue, Chicago, Ill. 60614; tel. 312/281-9075 or 800/331-6197). Distributes feature films in a variety of languages (90–120 minutes, $20–$80); language-learning tapes in Arabic, French, German, Italian, Japanese, Russian, and Spanish (90 minutes, $74.95); Berlitz language-learning tapes in French, German, Italian, and Spanish ($59.95).

FACSEA (972 Fifth Avenue, New York, N.Y. 10021; tel. 212/570-4400). This wing of the French Cultural Services has recently begun to include video material in its catalogues, including *Apostrophes* and various other programs (various lengths, reasonable prices).

Films for the Humanities, Inc. (Box 2053, Princeton, N.J. 08543; tel. 609/452-1128 or 800/257-5126). Concentrates on well-made cultural documents: video versions of Molière plays (52–140 minutes, $199–$249 purchase, $65 rental), nineteenth-century classics by Balzac, Flaubert, and Maupassant (52–99 minutes, $199 purchase, $75 rental), twentieth-century plays (45–110 minutes, $199 purchase, $65 rental), and French cultural topics (22–60 minutes, $149–$199 purchase, $65–$75 rental).

Films Incorporated–Education (1213 Wilmette Avenue, Wilmette, Ill. 60091; tel. 312/256-3200 or 800/323-4222). Distributes the entire BBC series of language-learning methods: *Everyday Mandarin, Deutsch Direkt, A Vous la France, Dicho y Hecho, Zarabanda, Buongiorno Italia!, Russian Language and People, Greek Language and People* (series vary from 250 to 625 minutes, prices average $125 per 25-minute program). Student textbooks and other ancillaries available for all series from EMC Publishing (see entry). Films Inc. also distributes other foreign-language video materials, such as the French adventure serial *La Marée et ses secrets* and numerous feature films. Films Inc. offers cable rights to many of its programs.

German Language Video Center (7625 Pendleton Pike, Indianapolis, Ind. 46226; tel. 317/547-1257). Primarily distributors of German feature films in NTSC or PAL (some without subtitles), priced from $30 to $90. Also available are travelogues, some German and Austrian TV series, and a few programs for younger viewers.

Gessler Publishing Co., Inc. (900 Broadway, New York, N.Y. 10003-1291; tel. 212/673-3113). Distributes French commercials (55 minutes,

$50), features on famous monuments (60 minutes, $70), a program of French folk dancing (55 minutes, $50). In German are commercials (25 minutes, $45), a complete German-language program (60 minutes, $195 with textbook, workbook, and audio cassettes), and German folk dancing (55 minutes, $50). Spanish offerings include folk dancing (55 minutes, $60) and cultural and travelogue programs (25–57 minutes, $40–$60). Gessler also distributes the Living Language video programs ($35 per program).

Goethe Institute, Embassy of the Federal Republic of Germany (4645 Reservoir Road, NW, Washington, D.C. 20007; tel. 202/298-4000, ext. 323). The West German government has been extremely helpful in making film and video materials available to American teachers of German. The catalogue of available materials changes regularly. Check with your closest Goethe Institute for availability.

Hachette (79, boulevard Saint-Germain, F-75288 Paris Cedex 06). Two video products are included in the Hachette line. *Avec Plaisir* is a complete language-teaching method contained on four videocassettes (also available on a PAL-SECAM videodisc). Each of thirteen lessons includes an episode of an ongoing story, as well as specifically targeted pedagogical sequences. Accompanying the video are a 176-page text, a workbook, and audiotapes keyed both to the book and to the videotapes. Hachette is also the original publisher of *97 publicités télévisées,* now distributed in the United States by D. C. Heath along with a matching workbook (see D. C. Heath and Company).

Hatier-Didier, U.S.A., Inc. (3160 "O" Street, NW, Washington, D.C. 20007; tel. 202/333-4435). Distributors of Jean Noël Rey's *Un Village dans Paris* (100 minutes, $200), as well as a digest of fifteen interviews from the same program, entitled *Portraits* (45 minutes, $100).

Heath: see D. C. Heath.

Heinle & Heinle (20 Park Plaza, Boston, Mass. 02116; tel. 617/451-1940 or 800/237-0053). Distributors of two videotapes made in France, Quebec, and Louisiana by Bernard Petit with native speakers: *The French Way* for the first year (60 minutes, $150) and *France from Within* for the intermediate level (60 minutes, $150). A workbook is also available.

Houghton Mifflin Company (One Beacon Street, Boston, Mass. 02108; tel. 617/725-5000). Distributes a number of authentic Spanish programs from the archives of Radio Televisión Española, including telefilms, interviews, music, ads, sports, and documentaries on Spanish and Latin American topics (17–60 minutes, $40–$80; reduced prices for adopters of Houghton Mifflin textbooks); either a video guide or a workbook by Rita Goldberg accompanies the Spanish videos. Distributes two episodes from a German television series *Ein kurzes Leben lang* (26 minutes, $60 each; reduced prices for adopters of Houghton Mifflin textbooks); a video guide by David Stout accompanies the German videos. Also distributes a videotape of twenty-six, 30-second French television commercials and public service announcements to accompany *Traits d'union* by Hester/Wade/Jian; suggestions for using French videotape appear in Instructor's Edition and Manual; Regional College Sales Offices: Texas, 800/558-8398, Illinois 800/323-5663, California 800/992-5121, New Jersey 800/445-6575.

International Film Bureau, Inc. (322 South Michigan Ave., Chicago, Ill. 60604-4382, 312/427-4545). One of the oldest educational audiovisual distributors, this corporation carries geographical features and short cultural subjects in Spanish (10-minute programs priced at $195, 20-minute programs at $250); songs, short tales, cultural vignettes, a series on food and wine from France, and features on art in French (7–59 minutes, $145–$675); the *Guten Tag* series, short geographical subjects, and art features in German (5–79 minutes, $120–$695); and an animated series and a few cultural films in Russian (9–14 minutes, $175–$195). Programs may be rented from College Film Center (see entry) as well as other regional depositories (audiovisual centers or instructional media services at the Universities of Arizona, Southern California, Utah, Illinois, Wisconsin, Michigan, Minnesota, and Connecticut, as well as Indiana, Boston, and Syracuse Universities).

Jem Communications, Inc. (Box 708, South Plainfield, N.J. 07080; tel. 201/753-6100 or 800/338-4814). Distributes *France Panorama,* a bimonthly summary of French news (60 minutes per tape on a subscription basis, $149.40 for six months, $274.80 for 12 months), and *Ecco l'Italia,* a bimonthly Italian video magazine (60 minutes per tape on a subscription basis, $149.40 for six months, $274.80 for twelve months). Language-learning guide included with each tape. Tapes also available with English subtitles.

The Media Guild (11722 Sorrento Valley Road, Suite E, San Diego, Calif. 92121-1021; tel. 619/755-9191). Distributes BBC and Thames Television programs in French on Paris and specific French institutions (18–20 minutes, $198) and in German (20 minutes, $198).

Middlebury College (*La Télé des Français,* Middlebury College Language Schools, Middlebury, Vt. 05753; tel. 802/388-3711, ext. 5685). Distributors of *La Télé des Français,* three cassettes of programs from French network television, including game shows, documentaries on gastronomy and the stock market, features on the painters Manet and Rousseau, a talent show, and a narrative fiction program (118 minutes per cassette, $130 per cassette or $350 for all three).

Mohawk Instructional Center (6649 Lamar, Shawnee Mission, Ka. 66202; tel. 913/384-6800, ext. 207). Distributes *Quoi de Neuf? Resources for the Teacher of French,* a videotape prepared by Jean Piel of the Shawnee Mission Public Schools, in conjunction with the Cultural Services of the Ministry of Education of France, presenting selections from currently available tapes in French (27 minutes, exchanged for a blank videotape).

National Film Board of Canada (1251 Avenue of the Americas, New York, N.Y. 10020; tel. 212/586-5131). Distributes French-language feature-length documentaries (purchase $350, rental $60).

PICS: see Project for International Communication Studies.

Polyglot Productions (136 Brattle Street, Cambridge, Mass. 02138; tel. 617/491-3541). Distributes foreign feature films, some without subtitles ($30–$130), as well as a selection of other foreign-language programs, including songs, cartoons, and some children's programming. Emphasis on French.

Project for International Communication Studies (PICS) (International Center, University of Iowa, Iowa City, Iowa 52242; tel. 319/335-2335 or 800/ALL-CALL, ext. INTV). PICS distributes a broad selection of programs in various languages (all cassettes are priced at $29.95 for 30 minutes or $39.95 for 60 minutes, with a 6-percent charge for mailing). General programming includes European newscasts co-produced with the BBC (*Telejournal*). French programming comes from Antenne 2 (*Panorama,* a monthly news digest, as well as numerous short documentaries and reports on contemporary topics), the Institut pour la Coopération Audiovisuelle Francophone, or ICAF (*Espace Francophone,* more than two dozen 26-minute programs on French-speaking countries), and the Centre National de Documentation Pédagogique, or CNDP (series on French for Beginners, France Today, Métiers Traditionnels, Marginal Groups, Medieval Civilization, Literary Authors, Les Jeunes, Business French, Justice—French Style, and the like). German programs range from features on classic authors to German news and business German. Videodiscs now available include carefully chosen selections from German and French news coverage with simplified second sound tracks and an introduction to economics with sound tracks in French and German. PICS includes a free teaching package with many of its tapes, including summary, partial transcript, exercises, and suggestions for use.

Tamarelle's International Films, Ltd. (110 Cohasset Stage Road, Chico, Calif. 95926; tel. 916/895-3429 or 800/356-3577 for orders). Primarily a distributor of feature-length films, initially in French and now in numerous languages. Most films are subtitled, but a few can be obtained without subtitles. A few fine arts programs are also available. Prices range from $30 to $90 for feature films (plus postage). Tamarelle's also runs a video exchange program (initial fee, including first cassette, is $79; each exchange costs $15).

Vedette Visuals (4820 58th Avenue West, Tacoma, Wash. 98466; tel. 206/564-4960). Distributes feature films in French, German, Italian, Japanese, Russian, and Spanish (purchase $35–$100, rental $23.50 per week).

Every effort has been made to assure the accuracy of this list. Notice of inaccuracies or omissions should be sent to the author care of the publisher. Appropriate corrections or additions will be made in subsequent editions of this book.

CONCLUSION
The Video of the
F̶u̶t̶u̶r̶e̶ Present

Inexpensive, flexible, and easy to manipulate, the videocassette recorder provides educators with a nearly perfect instrument. *Nearly* perfect: what a catalyst a single adverb can be! Throughout the past decade, efforts have been made around the world to give video technology the last bit of control or definition needed to achieve perfection. Many recent innovations may never be widely accepted or available within educational circles, but some are already operational in certain privileged institutions. For most instructors, therefore, these novelties represent the video of the future, whereas for a few they are the video of the present. By and large, four areas promise to contribute most directly to foreign-language video pedagogy: the videodisc, computer-controlled video, new methods of encoding and displaying video images, and increased availability of video programs.

In many ways the videodisc is no more than a rearranged videocassette, with the images all laid out next to each other in one enormous montage, rather than in succession, as in a thick photo album. With a videocassette you must page through hundreds of snapshots in order to find the right one. With a videodisc your eyes go right to the appropriate picture. By radically reducing the time it takes to gain access to any particular sequence, the videodisc opens up new instructional possibilities. Most videodisc systems permit reference to individual images by a specific frame number, which permits the user to locate a specific scene or even an individual image rapidly and accurately. Exercises involving comparison of images are thus greatly facilitated by a videodisc player with a hand controller. This technology is especially appropriate for activities that require rapid location of desired images—for example, the successive location of different postures or attitudes during an exercise on body language.

The accurate-to-the-frame control available with videodisc has always been available with professional videotape systems, which permit accurate time coding of each frame. It is no surprise, then, that even before the widespread availability of the videodisc medium, videocassette recorders were being interfaced with computers in order to provide perfect control and interactive use of the computer/VCR pair. With the videodisc comes

This scene from one of the few currently available videodiscs specifically intended for language instruction is taken from *ABC der Wirtschaft*. This program features videodiscs with both French and German soundtracks.

a significant reduction in the time required for computer-controlled video to access a specific frame, a development that makes interactive technology all the more attractive.[1] With computer-controlled videodiscs, the monitor instantly displays the output of the videodisc player and/or of the computer, with the computer controlling the videodisc player's movement. Images from videodisc and computer can be either alternated on the screen or, with a more sophisticated interface, overlaid so both are visible at once.

A cleverly written computer program can thus lead a student through a video program, stopping to ask appropriate questions, replaying segments for which the student's answer is inadequate, providing glosses for terms that the student fails to understand, and taking advantage of well-planned branching within either the video or the computer program. Students can learn at their own pace, with many of the benefits of teacher correction or counseling but without constant surveillance. This mode is ideal for individuals learning or reviewing a language independently.

Computer-controlled video applications will surely grow in number and importance when two recent innovations reach a wider market. Standard television systems have a maximum resolution of 525 lines for the NTSC standard and 625 lines for PAL and SECAM. New high-resolution television systems offer over a thousand lines, thus producing a far more detailed picture. In consequence, high-resolution television promises to open new perspectives for graphic applications useful to teachers of language. It will also raise projection television to far more acceptable quality levels. Even more important are new developments in digital video. Unlike traditional systems, digital video encodes visual information digitally, as a computer encodes information. Since digital video uses the same encoding system as a computer, it opens up vast new possibilities for computer/video interaction. Whereas traditional video images are virtually fixed once they have been made, digital images can easily be manipulated through computer control, thus creating new opportunities for combining language and image, computer and video.

For the language teacher, unfortunately, the advantages of the videodisc and other recent innovations remain more a dream than a reality. Lack of foreign-language programming on videodisc has made it hard in the past to justify the purchase of videodisc equipment.[2] Videodiscs pressed in the United States are in the NTSC standard, whereas most of the languages studied in American schools and colleges are spoken in countries that use the PAL or SECAM standard. Thus very few international foreign-language programs have been pressed on discs that can be played in the United States.[3] Several foreign-language discs have been produced in this country. Since many of these are experimental in nature, however, not all of them are available for sale.[4] Current interactive programs using international video materials, whether for tape or disc, are thus severely limited in number. By and large they come from a small number of American research and production centers: the Air Force Academy, Brigham Young University, the Defense Language Institute, MIT, the Monterey Institute of Foreign Studies, and the University of Iowa. As the number of available foreign-language videodiscs grows, along with the availability of videodisc players, there is every reason to expect that interactive videodisc programs will multiply rapidly. The technology is too flexible and too powerful for its educational potential to remain long untapped.

All the technology in the world, however, cannot engender a video-conscious pedagogy without a wide range of international programming. At present, available programs remain severely limited in number, type, and level. In the years to come, I look forward to an enormous growth in video catalogues. In recent years, we have seen an evolution in interest from video as a medium for recording the texts characteristic of another medium (the novel, theater, or cinema) to interest in the genres that are characteristic of television (news, weather, talk shows, publicity, short fiction, documentaries, information programs). We have also seen an increase in specially created videocassette programs (public relations programs, training films, self-contained courses). This expansion of available programming has occurred mostly in the college market. Many more programs should soon be directly aimed at junior-high and high-school courses, foreign language courses in the elementary schools, and immersion programs, as well as courses for advanced students in history, business, political science, and communication studies. In addition, languages and cultures heretofore unrepresented will be available on videocassette.

With plummeting prices and new developments in copying technology, along with new kinds of distribution agreements, it will soon be feasible to lend video programs to students, as audiotapes are lent in current tape-exchange programs. A new mode of publishing may already be evolving, in which video materials become the basis for textbooks or are conceived simultaneously with them. The sale of videotapes to students as basic course items is not far away.

To be sure, video programs alone will not change teaching practices. It is equally important to develop new strategies for video teaching. Today, there is a small but growing network of instructors who make major use of video in their classes. Many of them know one another and regularly trade insights and materials. Tomorrow there may be thousands more, eager to make international video materials work in and around the classroom. The birth of a serious and durable video pedagogy will be accelerated by active interchange among these video-conscious instructors. A nationwide network, already being developed by the Project for International Communication Studies, will facilitate the sharing of materials and approaches, not only throughout the United States but also in the countries where the target languages are spoken. In many cases, specialists in these countries have worked for years to develop successful strategies for teaching their language to foreigners.

There is nothing visionary in this assessment, no high-tech interactive technology required. The future envisioned here is already the present in educational centers around the country. With new materials available every month, with discs being pressed at an increasingly rapid pace and interactive programs in continuous development, the field of video pedagogy is bound to evolve. For the time being, we still need to concentrate on the basics, to learn more fully how to make video serve our educational purposes. I hope this book will contribute to that process.

Notes

1. On interactive video, see *The Educator's Handbook to Interactive Videodiscs,* 2nd ed. (Washington, D.C.: Association for Educational Communications and Technology, 1987). A special-interest group (SIGVIM) of the International Council for Computers in Education is dedicated

to educational uses of interactive video. For information, write ICCE-SIGVIM, University of Oregon, 1787 Agate Street, Eugene, Ore. 97403-9905.

2. Schools considering the purchase of videodisc equipment might profitably consult *Should Schools Use Videodiscs?*, a report from the Institute for the Transfer of Technology to Education, c/o James A. Mecklenburger, National School Boards Association, 1680 Duke Street, Alexandria, Va. 22314.

3. To my knowledge, the only current project to produce NTSC videodiscs featuring authentic foreign programs is sponsored by PICS, with the aid of the Annenberg/Corporation for Public Broadcasting Project. Initial programs in this series include German and French news selections, as well as an introduction to economics with French and German sound tracks.

4. The first and most influential of American-produced discs is certainly Brigham Young University's *Montevidisco*. More recent programs have been produced by researchers in the Athena project at MIT.

APPENDIX I
Glossary of Acronyms and Technical Terms

Antenne 2: leading French Television network.

audio dub: VCR feature that permits the user to replace original sound track with another (or add a second sound track) without disturbing the picture.

automatic zeroing: videocassette recorder feature that automatically stops tape when it reaches zero on counter (similar to *frame search* and *indexing*).

BBC: British Broadcasting Corporation, co-producer with PICS of *Telejournal*.

BELC: Bureau pour l'Enseignement de la Langue et de la Civilisation françaises à l'étranger, French organization that actively fosters video pedagogy.

Beta: 1/2″ videotape format used primarily by Sony VCRs.

branching: treelike structure used in computer programs (such as those used in computer-controlled video); provides for different question sequences according to student response.

Bravo: cable channel that carries many subtitled foreign films.

CAI: computer-assisted instruction.

CALICO: Computer Assisted Language Instruction Consortium.

CG: character generator, useful for adding titles to video programs.

Cinemax: cable channel that carries many subtitled foreign films.

Cloze: language-teaching method that requires students to complete a partial text.

computer-controlled videodisc: combination of computer, videodisc player, and interface that permits rapid access to and control over videodisc functions.

computer-controlled videotape: combination of computer, VCR, and interface that permits access to and control over VCR functions.

CPB: Corporation for Public Broadcasting, participant in the Annenberg/CPB Project and major supporter of *French in Action* and the Project for International Communication Studies.

digital video: system that defines each bit of information in a video image in such a way that it can be read or generated by a computer.

ESL: English as a second language.

extended-play mode: on videocassette recorders with multiple speeds, a slow speed that triples recording time.

FACSEA: French-American Cultural Services and Educational Aid.

fast forward and reverse: VCR feature that permits rapid movement, with no image visible, between parts of a videotape.

format: size and shape of videocassette.

frame search: VCR feature that permits rapid return to a predetermined spot on a videotape (similar to *automatic zeroing* and *indexing*).

1/2": most common size for videotape, used by VHS and Beta formats.

hand controller: remote control for some videodisc players.

headphone jack: outlet for attaching headphone to VCR, monitor, or television.

high-resolution television: television or video system capable of displaying especially detailed images; the resolution is over a thousand lines, compared with 525 for the NTSC standard and 625 for PAL and SECAM.

ICAF: Institut pour la Coopération Audiovisuelle Francophone, producers of the *Espace Francophone* series.

ICCE: International Council for Computers in Education.

indexing: VCR feature that permits automatic return to any of a number of predetermined spots on a tape (similar to *frame search* and *automatic zeroing*)

interface: necessary connector between computer and VCR or videodisc player; permits computer-controlled video operation.

kinesics: study of communication through bodily and other movement.

local-access channel: channel available for local programming on many cable systems.

master: file or archive copy of a video tape from which copies are made for student use.

MICEFA: Mission Interuniversitaire de Coordination des Echanges Franco-Américains, producers of the *Minibus/Maxifrench* series.

monitor: television-like apparatus for displaying video images that originate from a VCR or videodisc player; lacks tuner to receive television signal on its own.

multistandard monitor: monitor capable of displaying images in more than one standard.

multistandard VCR: VCR capable of playing videotapes recorded in more than one standard.

NTSC: National Television Standards Committee; designates television standard used in North America and parts of South America and East Asia.

off-air recording: recording from a broadcast or cable television signal.

PAL: Phase Alternate Line; designates television standard used in most of Europe and in parts of Africa, Asia, and South America.

pause: VCR feature that permits display of a still image from a videotape.

PICS: Project for International Communication Studies, nonprofit distributor of international video materials, located at the University of Iowa.

play mode: VCR mode in which videotape remains in contact with video heads; used for play, record, pause, and visible forward and reverse.

programmable recording: VCR feature that permits automatic off-air recording when no VCR operator is present.

projection video: apparatus that permits projection of a large video image on a wall or screen.

quick-start system: VCR feature that keeps videotape in permanent contact with video heads, thus permitting rapid access to image even after fast forward or reverse.

RAI: Radio Audizioni Italiana (Italian National Network), broadcasts Italian-language programs in some parts of the United States.

receiver: television, including tuner and monitor (as opposed to monitor, which has no tuner).

rewind mode: VCR mode in which videotape remains in cassette; used for stop, fast forward, and rewind.

RTVE: Radio Televisión Española, major Spanish video producer and archive.

satellite reception: reception of video programming relayed by satellite.

schema: previously acquired knowledge structures that viewers use as an aid in constructing the meaning of a currently viewed program.

SCOLA: Satellite Communications for Learning Worldwide, directed by Lee Lubbers, S. J., located at Creighton University; distributors of foreign television programming by satellite.

SECAM: Séquence de Couleurs avec Mémoire; designates television standard used in France, the U.S.S.R., and parts of Africa and Asia.

second sound track: feature that permits videotape to carry two different sound tracks.

SIGVIM: special-interest group of the ICCE, dedicated to educational uses of interactive video.

SIN: Spanish International Network, U.S. cable channel that features Spanish-language programming; now known as Univision.

standard: method of encoding video information (NTSC, PAL, SECAM).

standards conversion: system for making a copy of a videotape in a different standard from the original.

3/4″: common professional videotape size (U-Matic).

TPR: Total Physical Response, a language-teaching methodology developed by James J. Asher.

tracking control: adjustment that facilitates display on one VCR of a videotape recorded on another.

transcoding: popular term for standards conversion.

tuner: part of a television or VCR that permits reception of a program.

U-Matic: common 3/4″ format.

VCR: videocassette recorder.

VHS: most common 1/2″ format.

video cart: wheeled cart that permits easy movement of video equipment.

videodisc: disc that carries video images readable by videodisc player.

visible forward and reverse: VCR feature that permits rapid movement, with image visible, to another part of tape.

Vremya: U.S.S.R. news program, available by cable or satellite in some parts of the United States.

VTR: videotape recorder.

wireless remote control: remote device that permits control over VCR or TV functions.

APPENDIX II
Distributors of Video Programs Mentioned in the Text

Following the name of the program are the names of the U.S. distributor and the original source (in parentheses), the name of the series or frequency of distribution, and other pertinent information.

ABC de l'économie: PICS (Eurotel), available as a complete five-hour program on five cassettes with French sound track or as selections on a two-sided one-hour videodisc with French and German sound tracks.

ABC der Wirtschaft: PICS (Eurotel), available as a complete five-hour program on five cassettes with German sound track or as selections on a two-sided one-hour videodisc with French and German sound tracks.

Advertisements: see Publicity

Beynac, un château au moyen âge: PICS (CNDP), Medieval Civilization series.

Le Calife d'Argenteuil: PICS (CNDP), Les Jeunes series.

Le Casse de Clamart: PICS (CNDP), Justice—French Style series.

Les Chemins de la sérénité: Jean-Jacques Rousseau: PICS (CNDP), Literary Figures series.

Des Chiffres et des lettres: Middlebury College (France Media International), part of *La Télé des Français* I and III.

La Communauté européenne dans le monde: PICS (EEC), French PR Video series.

Connaître ses droits: PICS (CNDP), Business French series.

Delphine Delamare: PICS (CNDP), Literary Figures series.

D'hier à aujourd'hui: La population française: PICS (CNDP), France Today series.

Douze ans après: PICS (CNDP), France Today series.

Espace francophone: PICS (ICAF); twenty-six-program series.

Evocation médiévale: Semur-en-Auxois: PICS (CNDP), Medieval Civilization series.

Femmes immigrées: PICS (CNDP), Marginal Groups series.

Fleuve Sénégal: PICS (ICAF), part of Espace Francophone series.

France-Panorama: Jem (Antenne 2); bimonthly news program.

France-TV Magazine: University of Maryland–Baltimore County (Antenne 2); monthly one-hour program available by satellite.

French in Action: Annenberg/CPB Project complete video course.

Histoire de la poste: PICS (PTT), French PR Video series.

Isabelle et Véronique ou les deux lycéennes: PICS (CNDP), Les Jeunes series.

Johann Wolfgang von Goethe: PICS (Eurotel), Deutsche Dichter-Profile series.

Ein kurzes Leben lang: Houghton Mifflin (Norddeutscher Rundfunk), two episodes available.

Little Red Riding Hood: PICS (University of Iowa); both Perrault and Grimm versions are available with either French or German sound track.

La Main dans le sac: PICS (CNDP), Justice—French Style series.

Maupassant short stories: Films for the Humanities, Inc. (France Media International); several different stories available separately.

Miroir dentelé: PICS (PTT), French PR Video series.

Monastères du moyen âge: PICS (CNDP), Medieval Civilization series.

Monnaie et crédit: PICS (CNDP), Business French series.

Montaigne dans son labyrinthe: PICS (CNDP), Literary Figures series; written by Michel Butor.

Nachrichten I: PICS (BBC), available on cassette or videodisc, with original and simplified sound tracks.

Ni en vivo ni en directo: Houghton Mifflin (RTVE), part of Set I, Program 5, *Los Pajaritos.*

Panorama: PICS (Antenne 2); monthly news program.

Un paseo por Hispanoamérica: Houghton Mifflin (RTVE), part of Set II.

Le Petit Chaperon Rouge: PICS (University of Iowa); both Perrault and Grimm versions with French sound track.

La Porcelaine à Limoges: PICS (CNDP), Métiers Traditionnels series.

La Présidence de la République: PICS (CNDP), Civilization series.

La Production laitière: PICS (CNDP), Métiers Traditionnels series.

Publicity: French TV publicity is available from D. C. Heath (*97 Publicités télévisées*) and Gessler; German TV publicity is available from Gessler; Spanish TV publicity is available from Houghton Mifflin.

El pueblo sumergido: Houghton Mifflin (RTVE), part of Set I.

97 Publicités télévisées: D. C. Heath (Hachette).

Quechuas, Huicholes, Panameños: Houghton Mifflin (RTVE), part of Set II.

Radio Beur: PICS (CNDP), Marginal Groups series.

Regain: PICS (CNDP), Marginal Groups series.

Rotkäppchen: PICS (University of Iowa); both Grimm and Perrault versions with German sound track.

Sécurité Routière: PICS (CNDP), six programs in the French for Beginners series.

Semur-en-Auxois: see *Evocation médiévale: Semur-en-Auxois.*

La Soie façonnée à Lyon: PICS (CNDP), Métiers Traditionnels series.

Sur l'éducation des filles: PICS (CNDP), Les Jeunes series.

La Télé des Français: Middlebury College (France Media International).

Télé-douzaine: PICS (Antenne 2); news selection for second-year use.

Telejournal: PICS (BBC); weekly news program including selection of news from a different European TV station each week, with BBC introduction in English.

Télématin: PICS (Antenne 2); selection of material for first-year use from first French morning show (available in 1989).

Touche pas à mon pote: PICS (MICEFA); part of *Minibus/Maxifrench* series.

TV-France Magazine: see *France-TV Magazine.*

Vaches bien ordonnées: PICS (CNDP), France Today series.

VELVET: CALICO, also available on videodisc.

Venezolanos: Houghton Mifflin (RTVE), part of Set I, Program 4, *Desde Venezuela a la Patagonia.*

Victor Hugo et la révolution: PICS (CNDP), Literary Figures series.

Un Village se met à table: PICS (CNDP), France Today series.

Vivre femme: PICS (CNDP), Marginal Groups series.

Selected Bibliography

Albert, M.-C., and E. Bérard-Lavenne. "Documents télévisés et apprentissage linguistique." *Le Français dans le Monde,* 157 (November–December 1980), 99–105.

Altman, Rick. "Access to International Television." *Studies in Language Learning,* 5:1 (1985), 17–24.

Asher, James J. *Learning Another Language Through Actions: The Complete Teacher's Guidebook.* Los Gatos, Calif.: Sky Oaks Productions, 1977.

Aulestia, Victor H. "The Impact on a Foreign Language Curriculum of Foreign Language Television Signals from Geosynchronous Earth Satellites." *NALLD Journal,* 18:1 (1983), 21–23.

Bakker, Henry, et al. *Technology in the Curriculum: Foreign-Language Resource Guide.* Sacramento, Calif.: California State Department of Education, 1987.

Berwald, Jean-Pierre. "The Videotape Recorder as a Teaching Aid." *French Review,* 43:6 (1970), 923–27.
———. "Teaching French Language Skills with Commercial Television." *French Review,* 50:2 (December 1976), 222–26.
———. "Teaching Foreign Language Skills by Means of Subtitled Visuals." *Foreign Language Annals,* 12:5 (1979), 375–80.
———. "Teaching French via Driver Education." *Foreign Language Annals,* 13:5 (1980), 205–08.
———. "Video and Second Language Learning." *Studies in Language Learning,* 5:1 (1985), 3–16.
———. *Au Courant: Teaching French Vocabulary and Culture Using the Mass Media.* Washington, D.C.: Center for Applied Linguistics, 1986. See especially Chapter 12, "Commercial Television."

Billings, R. D. "Off-the-Air Videorecording, Face-to-Face Teaching, and the 1976 Copyright Act." *Northern Kentucky Law Review,* 4 (1977), 225–51.

Birckbichler, D. W. *Creative Activities for the Second-Language Classroom.* Washington, D.C.: Center for Applied Linguistics, 1982.

Blakely, Richard. *Filmodule I (La Bête humaine), II (Pépé le Moko), III (La Grande Illusion)*. Rumford, R.I.: Professional Language Associates, 1981.

British Journal of Language Teaching. Special issue, "The Use of Broadcast Material in Language Teaching." Vol. 18, no. 2/3 (Winter 1980).

Brumfit, C., ed. *Video Applications in Language Teaching*. London: Pergamon, 1983.

Buehler, G. "The Videotape Recorder in Foreign Language Conversation and Composition Courses." *Foreign Language Annals*, 15:2 (1983), 103–107.

Bufe, W. "L'enseignement des langues à l'université à l'aide de la télévision." *Etudes de linguistique appliquée*, 38 (1980), 119–44.

Chung, Ulric. "An Introduction to Interactive Video." *Studies in Language Learning*, 5:1 (1985), 97–104.

Compte, Carmen. "Professeur cherche document authentique en vidéo." *Etudes de linguistique appliquée*, 58 (1985).

Compte, Carmen, and J. Mouchon. *Décoder le journal télévisé*. Paris: BELC, 1984.

Compte, Carmen, et al. *La Main dans le sac*. Paris: BELC, 1986.

Crouse, G., and B. A. Noll. "Using Videotapes to Teach Foreign Languages." *Foreign Language Annals*, 13 (1980), 391–93.

Danahy, Michael. "TV or Not TV?" *Studies in Language Learning*, 5:1 (1985), 53–60.

De Margerie, C., and Louis Porcher. *Des Médias dans les cours de langue*. Paris: Clé International, 1981.

Donchin, Rita. "Video in Language Learning." *Studies in Language Learning*, 5:1 (1985), 61–66.

Ecklund, Constance L. "Parody and Phonetics: Video in the Conversation Class." *Studies in Language Learning*, 5:1 (1985), 67–76.

Ecklund, C. L., and P. Wiese. "French Accent Through Video Analysis." *Foreign Language Annals*, 14:1 (1981), 17–23.

Foreign Language Audiovisuals. Albuquerque, N.M.: National Information Center for Educational Media, 1986.

Garrity, Henry A. *Film in the French Classroom*. Cambridge, Mass.: Polyglot, 1987.

Geddes, M., and G. Strudbridge, eds. *Video in the Language Classroom*. London: Heinemann, 1982.

Gillespie, Junetta B. "Self-Produced Video Tapes in Second Language Instruction." *Studies in Language Learning,* 5:1 (1985), 29–34.
————, ed. "Video and Second Language Learning." Special issue of *Studies in Language Learning,* 5:1 (Spring 1985).

Glass, E., and J. Fiedler-Glass. "Videotape in Language Instruction: A Brief Survey and an Annotated Bibliography of Spanish and Bilingual Videotapes." *Bilingual Review,* 1:1 (1974), 124–36.

Goldberg, Rita. *Video Guide.* Guide to accompany videocassettes from Radio Televisión Española. Boston: Houghton Mifflin Company, 1985.

Goodman, Pearl. "Video in Second Language Teacher Training." *Studies in Language Learning,* 5:1 (1985), 77–82.

Hill, J. K. "The Recording and Use of Off-Air French Television Programmes." *Audio-Visual Language Journal,* 16:2 (1978), 81–84.

Honigsblum, Gerald. *97 publicités télévisées: le français en réclame.* Lexington, Mass.: D. C. Heath and Co., 1987.

Hudson, Thom. "The Effects of Induced Schemata on the 'Short Circuit' in L2 Reading: Non-Decoding Factors in L2 Reading Performance." *Language Learning,* 32 (1982), 1–31.

Jacquinot, Geneviève. *Image et pédagogie: Analyse sémiologique du film à intention didactique.* Paris: Presses Universitaires de France, 1977.
————. *L'Ecole devant les écrans.* Paris: Presses Universitaires de France, 1985.

Jensen, E. "Video in Foreign Language Teaching." *System,* 6:1 (1978), 25–29.

Jensen, E., and T. Vithner. "Authentic Versus Easy Conflict in Foreign Language Material—a Report on Experiences with Production and Exploitation of Video in FLT." *System,* 7:2 (1983), 261–75.

Keilstrup, D. "Using the Situation-oriented Miniplay and VTR in Advanced Conversation Classes." *Foreign Language Annals,* 13 (1980), 367–70.

Knight, M. "Video in Oral Proficiency Training." *System,* 3:2 (1975), 81–83.

Knox, Edward, and François Mariet, eds. *La Télé des Français.* Pedagogical supplement to videocassettes from French television. Middlebury, Vt.; Middlebury College, 1985.

Krashen, Stephen D. *Principles and Practice in Second Language Acquisition.* New York: Pergamon, 1982.

Krashen, Stephen D., and Tracy Terrell. *The Natural Approach: Language*

Acquisition in the Classroom. San Francisco: Alemany Press; London: Pergamon, 1983.

Lancien, Thierry. *Le Document vidéo dans la classe de langues*. Paris: Clé International, 1986.

Langue Française. Special issue, "Audiovisuel et enseignement du français." No. 24 (1974).

Lawrence, Katherine D. "The French TV Commercial as a Pedagogical Tool in the Classroom." *French Review,* 60:6 (May 1987), 835–44.

Lebel, P. *Audiovisuel et pédagogie*. Paris: ESF, 1984.

Lonergan, Jack. *Video in Language Teaching*. Cambridge: Cambridge University Press, 1984.

Lubbers, Lee, S.J. "Satellite Reception of Foreign Language Programming." *Studies in Language Learning,* 5:1 (1985), 25–28.

Mainous, Bruce H., with Robert L. Blomeyer, Jr., and Junetta B. Gillespie. "Spanish for Agricultural Purposes: Another Use of Video." *Studies in Language Learning,* 5:1 (1985), 83–96.

Marchessou, François. "Vidéo et enseignement du français à l'université." *Le français dans le monde,* 158 (January 1981), 72–74.

McCoy, I. H., and D. M. Weible. "Foreign Languages and the New Media: The Videodisc and the Microcomputer." In *Practical Applications of Research in Foreign Language Teaching*. Ed. C. J. James. Lincolnwood, Ill.: National Textbook Company, 1983.

Miller, Jerome K. *Using Copyrighted Videocassettes in Classrooms and Libraries*. Champaign, Ill.: Copyright Information Services, 1984.

Mueller, G. A. "Visual Contextual Cues and Listening Comprehension: An Experiment." *Modern Language Journal,* 64:3 (1980), 335–40.

Normand, G. "Motivating with Media: The Use of Video at the Elementary and Intermediate Level in High School and College." *Canadian Modern Language Review/Revue Canadienne des Langues Vivantes,* 37:1 (1980): 51–55.

Odum, William. "The Use of Videotape in Foreign Language Instruction: A Survey." *NALLD Journal,* 10:3/4 (1976), 73–81.

Olivier, Louis A. "Using 'Off-Air' Television Broadcasts from Non-U.S. Sources—Some Practical Suggestions." *Studies in Language Learning,* 5:1 (1985), 45–52.

Omaggio, Alice C. *Teaching Language in Context: Proficiency-Oriented Instruction*. Boston: Heinle & Heinle, 1986.

Reed, Mary Hutchings, and Debra Stanek. "Library and Classroom Use of Copyrighted Videotapes and Computer Software." Center insert in *American Libraries,* 17:2 (1981), 5–13.

Rivers, Wilga. *Teaching Foreign Language Skills.* 2nd ed. Chicago: University of Chicago Press, 1981.

Santoni, G. V. "Using Videotape in the Advanced Conversation Class." *Foreign Language Annals,* 8 (1975), 233–38.

Shubin, Mark. "Bon Video Voyage, 7 Myths about Foreign TV." *Video Review,* 4:6 (1983), 44–46.

Silva, T. "Teacher-made Videotape Materials for the Second-Language Classroom." *Studies in Language Learning,* 4:2 (1983), 128–43.

Sinofsky, Esther R. *Off-Air Videotaping in Education: Copyright Issues, Decisions, Implications.* New York: R. R. Bowker, 1984.

Skirble, R. "Television Commercials in the Foreign Language Classroom." *Hispania,* 60:3 (1977), 516–18.

Stout, David F. *Video Guide.* Guide to accompany *Ein Kurzes Leben lang* (videos from Norddeutscher Rundfunk and Studio Hamburg Atelier G.m.b.H.) Boston: Houghton Mifflin Company, 1985.

Tanner, Jacquelyn. "Where's the Video—a Review of Sources for Foreign Languages." *Studies in Language Learning,* 5:1 (1985), 35–44.

INDEX

Page numbers in italics refer to illustrations

DEMO VIDEO

In collaboration with Houghton Mifflin, the Project for International Communication Studies (PICS) has prepared a VHS demo tape to accompany THE VIDEO CONNECTION. This 30-minute tape contains excerpts from many of the video sequences discussed in THE VIDEO CONNECTION.

If you would like to receive a copy of this tape, please fill out the forms below and send them to:

> The Project for International Communication Studies
> 266 International Center
> University of Iowa
> Iowa City, IA 52242

Name: _____

Department: _____

School: _____

Address: _____

City/State/Zip: _____

Please note that this offer is limited to one video tape per school.

Enclose $5.00 to cover shipping and handling. All orders must be prepaid.

Name:_____

Department:_____

Language(s) taught:_____

School:_____

Address:_____

City/State/Zip:_____